STUDY GUIDE
For Individuals and Adult Groups

The Unshakable TRUTH™

JOSH McDOWELL
SEAN McDOWELL

HARVEST HOUSE PUBLISHERS

EUGENE, OREGON

TAUCHER - 651-773-9468

THE UNSHAKABLE TRUTH™ STUDY GUIDE
Copyright © 2010 by Josh McDowell Ministry and Sean McDowell
Published by Harvest House Publishers
Eugene, Oregon 97402
www.harvesthousepublishers.com

ISBN 978-0-7369-3053-6

Printed in the United States of America

10 11 12 13 14 15 16 17 18 / BP-NI / 10 9 8 7 6 5 4 3 2 1

CONTENTS

About the Authors

Authors Josh and Sean McDowell collaborated with their writer to bring you this study guide. The content is based upon the McDowells' book *The Unshakable Truth*.

Over 45-plus years, **Josh McDowell** has spoken to more than 10 million people in 115 countries about the evidence for Christianity and the difference the Christian faith makes in the world. He has authored or coauthored more than 115 books (with more than 51 million copies in print), including such classics as *More Than a Carpenter* and *New Evidence That Demands a Verdict*.

Sean McDowell is an educator and a popular speaker at schools, churches, and conferences nationwide. He is author of *Apologetics for a New Generation* and *Ethix: Being Bold in a Whatever World,* coauthor of *Understanding Intelligent Design,* and general editor of *The Apologetics Study Bible for Students.* He is currently pursuing a PhD in apologetics and worldview studies.

About the Writer

Writer Dave Bellis developed the outline of the video production and study guide course and wrote this study guide based upon Josh and Sean's book *The Unshakable Truth*.

Dave Bellis is a ministry consultant focusing on ministry planning and product development. He is a writer, producer, and product developer. He and his wife, Becky, have two grown children and live in northeastern Ohio.

Acknowledgments

We would like to thank the many people who brought creativity and insight to forming this study guide and video production:

Terri Snead and David Ferguson of Great Commandment Network for their writing insights for the TruthTalk and Truth Encounter sections of this study guide.

Shane White of Harvest House for his production and management skills in producing the video elements that go with this study.

Jeanna Minshall, Steve Coker, and their professional team at Chambers Productions of Eugene, Oregon, for shooting and post-producing the final video product.

Terry Glaspey for his insights and guidance as he helped in the development of the study guide lessons.

Paul Gossard for his skillful editing of the study guide manuscript.

And finally, the entire team at Harvest House, who graciously endured the process with us.

Josh McDowell
Sean McDowell
Dave Bellis

WE'VE GOT A QUESTION FOR YOU

We've actually got three questions for you. You are about to begin *The Unshakable Truth Study Guide*. And by knowing the answers to these three questions, you can get the most out of this material.

1. Who Is This For?

This study guide is for anyone who wants to make real sense out of Christianity. What is the Christian faith all about anyway? What defines it, what does God want from us individually, and how do we pass the faith on to our families, friends, and others?

This may sound strange, but most Christians don't know the answers to those questions. If you want answers and want to know what being a Christian really means, this study provides an excellent introduction to the foundations of the faith.

2. How Does It Work?

There are 12 truths that make up what Christianity is all about. Whether you are using this guide individually or in a group, you will find questions to answer, issues to think through, and truths to apply to your life. To enhance your study experience there are two optional ways to view videos of Josh and Sean McDowell discussing each truth:

1. You can go to a special website (www.unshakabletruth.com/sg) to view 15 to 17 minutes of teaching per session from Josh and Sean at no cost.

2. You can purchase a high-resolution DVD more suitable for group use. The DVD contains 12 sessions—the same sessions available on the website.

Whichever route you choose, this video feature will provide an enhanced study experience for your group or for you individually.

As you go through each truth, exploring Scripture, answering questions, and watching video segments, you will uncover what makes being a follower of Christ unique and fulfilling. Because this study is based on Josh and Sean's book *The Unshakable Truth,* we suggest you obtain the book for supplemental reading. You can order the book directly from the publisher by calling 1-800-547-8979 or order online at HarvestHousePublishers.com/UnshakableTruth.

3. Where Is This Going?

The Unshakable Truth Study Guide is just the beginning. It deals with each truth in an introductory fashion, highlighting the key points of *The Unshakable Truth* book, which deals with the 12 core truths of the Christian faith in 51 chapters.

As a follow-up, the TruthWalk courses take each truth and examine it in depth to cover

1. what we believe about each truth
2. why we can believe each one with confidence
3. how each one is relevant to life
4. how to live out each truth so you can impart your faith to your family, friends, and others

In brief, the TruthWalk courses are a media-assisted interactive group experience of the book *The Unshakable Truth.* The TruthWalk journey is like a Christian catechism to equip you for a lifelong pattern of spiritual and relational growth.

The study guide you are using now will open your heart and mind to a whole new way of living. The TruthWalk courses will lead you on a deepened and long-term journey of commitment to Christ, and you will discover along the way how to impart your faith to your family and those around you. The flexibility of these courses allows you to take your time to explore how you were meant to live God's truths out in community with family and your committed brothers and sisters in Christ. (For more information about TruthWalk go to www.HarvestHouse Publishers.com/TruthWalk.)

But first things first. You are now ready to start with the first session of *The Unshakable Truth Study Guide*. So let your journey begin!

TRUTH ONE: GOD EXISTS

What Are We Talking About?

To help you frame some important questions about God's existence, consider the following excerpt from chapter 4 of *The Unshakable Truth* book:

"*We live on Planet Earth, which is part of a vast universe. And it's natural to ask where we all came from and for what purpose we exist. Our home on earth seems so insignificant and small, suspended as it is in the vastness of space. Is God out there somewhere in the vastness? Think about space for a moment. It seems to stretch on and on without any possibility of ending. When we try to imagine the size even of the known universe, it's impossible to truly comprehend. But let's try.*

"*The expanses of the universe are so immense that we measure them using the light-year, which is the distance light travels in 365 days. Light travels at the speed of 186,282 miles per second. In a year, that distance, multiplied out and rounded off, increases to 5,865,696,000,000, almost 6 trillion, miles. To put that in a perspective we can almost grasp, it takes a sunbeam just over 8 minutes to travel the 93 million miles from the sun to earth. So what is the size of the observable universe in terms of light-years? Scientists say matter is spread over a space at least 93 billion light-years across. Our Milky Way galaxy is roughly 100,000 light years in diameter. Its nearest sister galaxy, the Andromeda galaxy, is located roughly 2.5 million light years away. And there are probably more than 100 billion galaxies in the observable universe.*

"*As finite beings we simply cannot imagine such distances, such magnitude. And the very concept of infinite space is far more than our minds can handle. How was this vast space formed, and why? Could it all be here just by chance? And if not, how can we know why we are here?*"

As a child, did you ever wonder where you came from? Complete the following sentence.

"I asked _____ *where I came from and he or she told me...*

_____

_____

_____ *."*

You may have proof of your family identity by a birth certificate, but what proof do you have that God created everything? How would you answer someone who asked, "How do you know God created all that there is?"

_____

_____

_____

||||||||||||||||||||||||||||||||||||||||||||||||||||||||||||||||||||||||||||||||||||||||||||||||||||||||

Session Objective

To gain a greater devotion to and understanding of our Creator God and why he created us.

Notice: As explained in the introduction of this guide, to enhance your study experience there are two optional ways to view videos of Josh and Sean McDowell discussing each truth. To view the video segments free of charge via the web go to www.unshakabletruth .com/sg and follow the instructions below. If you prefer to purchase a high-resolution DVD more suitable for group use you may place your order on the website.

Video

So, if you elect to use the DVD or web links, view Session One, Part 1 now. This video is a 5-minute segment of Josh and Sean introducing this truth. The online session is at **www.unshakabletruth.com/sg**. Click on "Video Menu" and then " Session One, Part 1."

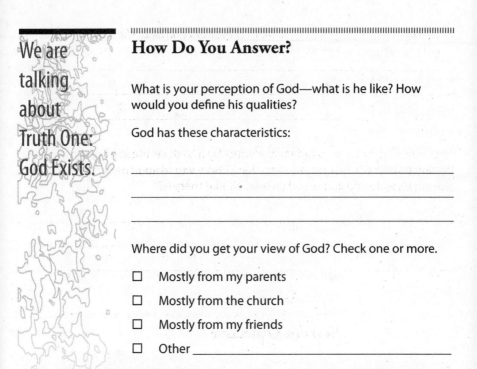

We are talking about Truth One: God Exists.

How Do You Answer?

What is your perception of God—what is he like? How would you define his qualities?

God has these characteristics:

_____

_____

_____

Where did you get your view of God? Check one or more.

☐ Mostly from my parents

☐ Mostly from the church

☐ Mostly from my friends

☐ Other _____

Many people get their view of God based on the dominant authority figure from their childhood. Is that true of you? Who was that person, and how accurately did he or she reflect who God is?

_____

_____

Notice: Each video part 2 begins by repeating the on-the-street interviews.

 Video

Now play DVD Session One, Part 2, or go back to the website **www.unshakabletruth.com/sg** to view an 11-minute conversation on this subject by Josh and Sean. Again, click first on "Video Menu" and then "Session One, Part 2."

Truth One: God Exists

We believe the truth that there is an infinite, personal God of the universe.

How It Applies

If you have children, what view of God do they have? Do you sense that your child's view of God reflects the child-parent relationship the two of you have? In what way?

_____

_____

_____

Read Genesis 1:26-27. The identifying marker or distinguishing characteristic of God's image and likeness that we carry is the capacity for loving relationships. So how would you define the basic idea of *relationship?* In other words,

"Relationship *to me means...*

_____

_____

_____."

Read Genesis 2:18 and 23-24. What does this passage indicate relationship does for you?

_____

_____

_____

God created each of us for relationship with him and one another. How do relationships remove our human aloneness and give us a sense of completeness and meaning? *"Relationships remove our aloneness and give us a sense of completeness when...*

_____

_____

_____."

Scripture gives us at least two insights into the way relationships remove our human aloneness.

Read Jeremiah 1:5. "To know" in this verse is the Hebrew word *yada,* and it denotes deep and intimate acquaintance. How does it make you feel when someone wants to know you for who you are? When someone knows you intimately, it deepens your relationship with him or her because...

_____

_____

_____

Read Proverbs 3:32. "Friendship" in this verse is the Hebrew word *sod,* meaning vulnerable or transparent disclosure. God has openly revealed himself to us through Jesus, and he wants us to open ourselves up and be vulnerable to one another.

Why do we sometimes hesitate to be transparent and open with others? In other words,

"I am sometimes hesitant to be open with others because...

_____

_____

_____ *."*

The relational image of God is all about knowing and being known. The more we seek to know another person for who they truly are and reveal ourselves to them, the deeper our relationships will become.

|||||||||||||||||||||||||||||||||||||||||||||||||||||||||||||||||||||||||||||||||||||||||||||||||||||||||||||||||||||||||

Truth Encounter

Read Jeremiah 1:5.

Take a few moments to meditate on Jeremiah 1:5. Reflect on the truth that the sovereign God of the universe knows you. The same God who created our Milky Way, as well as the 100 billion other galaxies of our universe—knows you. He knows everything about you—your faults and failures, uncertainties and inadequacies, your good days and bad ones—and still he loves you deeply, intimately, and thoroughly. He loves you with an everlasting love!

Pause quietly and think about this amazing truth. Allow the Spirit to lead you as you consider this: The One who knows you the most, loves you the best! How does your heart respond?

_____

_____

_____

_____

God has made himself vulnerable by sharing his Son and his love with you. Could you make yourself vulnerable by sharing with him? Could you share your gratitude with him? Your praise, thanks, or worship?

"Dear God, as I reflect on both your knowing of me and loving me, my heart is moved

with _____. *And I want to tell you…*

_____

_____

_____

_____."

(For example: "My heart is moved with thanks. And I want to tell you that I would like to know you better and love you more.")

If you are in a small group, share the sentence you wrote above with the others.

Truth Talk—An Assignment for the Week

The apostle Paul wrote:

"We loved you so much that we gave you not only God's Good News but our own lives, too" (1 Thessalonians 2:8-9).

Consider the following ideas and make plans to initiate a spiritual conversation this week with someone, particularly those in your family. Share any insight you have had as you've encountered God's truth. Relationally share a part of yourself. If you have a child or teenager, make sure to prioritize a time to start these spiritual conversations with them. Consider saying something like:

1 "I've been going through *The Unshakable Truth Study Guide.* I've been learning how the same God who created the entire universe knows us and loves us. I've been especially moved by that truth because…

_____

_____."

 2 "I've been concerned recently about my struggle with…

_____

(my temper, unforgiveness, discouragement, gossip, or something else) and I've been so grateful to realize the truth that God knows all about my struggle, loves me anyway, and is working to change me!"

3 "As I look back at the path of my life with the various job opportunities and career moves, it sure seems like God knew exactly how my gifts and talents could best be used. It's amazing to me that the God who directs the universe can orchestrate the smallest details of my life! I can look back and see how…

_____

_____."

Ask God to provide an opportunity for you to share one or more of these TruthTalks with a friend, co-worker, child, teen, family member, or someone who needs Christ.

As a review read chapters 1–7 of *The Unshakable Truth* book this week and chapters 8–11 for the next session.

‖‖

Close Your Time in Prayer

Truth Two: God's Word

What Are We Talking About?

"The Bible. No other book has been so widely distributed in so many languages. According to the United Bible Society's report, in one year alone 28.4 million complete Bibles were distributed, as well as just under 300 million selections from the Bible. The Bible or portions of the Bible have been translated into more than 2400 languages. And amazingly, these languages represent the primary communication for well over 90 percent of the world's population."

What is your earliest recollection of seeing a Bible?

"I remember realizing the Bible existed when I was about _____ old. I remember I started reading the Bible for myself when I was _____."

But what is the Bible? *"I would describe the Bible as…*

_____

_____."*

And what does the Bible do for us? *"I would say…*

_____

_____."*

We are talking about Truth Two: God's Word

Session Objective

To discover the deeper meaning of God's Word in our lives and gain greater confidence that the Bible is reliable.

Video

If you are using the DVD or web links, view Session Two, Part 1. It is a 7-minute video of Josh and Sean introducing this truth. The online session is at **www.unshakabletruth .com/sg**. Click on "Video Menu" and then "Session Two, Part 1."

How Do You Answer?

Do you trust the Bible to be true and reliable? There's a reason you can trust the Bible to be reliable, and that is…

_____

_____

_____

Or, do you struggle with trusting the Bible to be reliable because…

_____

_____

_____

Read 2 Timothy 3:16-17. Based on this verse, what would you say the purpose of Scripture is in your life?

_____

_____

_____

The overarching role of Scripture is described in chapter 2 of *The Unshakable Truth* book:

"Far too many Christians see Scripture as merely a set of rules and teachings. They fail to see the Bible as an expression of who we are as God's creation, and our purpose for existence. Unlock the Scripture, and it provides a depiction of a specific way of life, a way of knowing what is true, a picture of being what God meant us to be, and a pattern of living based on the revelation of who God is in relationship to us. Or, to put it another way, Scripture reveals everything we need to know to see the truth about what the world was meant to be, what it is now, and how it can be restored to his original intention. Scripture shows us that we were originally designed to be in relationship with God, it shows what caused us to lose that relationship, and it shows how it can be reclaimed."

 Video

Now play DVD Session Two, Part 2, or go back to **www.unshakabletruth .com/sg** and click on "Video Menu" and then on "Session Two, Part 2" to view Josh and Sean discussing this truth for 10 minutes.

Truth Two: God's Word

We believe the truth that the Bible is God's revelation of himself to us, which declares his ways for us to follow.

How It Applies

Josh and Sean explained why we can trust the New Testament. But let's explore the Bible's reliability further.

What would the ramifications be if a scribe had failed to copy what had previously been written in a manuscript of the Hebrew Scriptures? What if someone copying the Greek manuscript had changed the Sermon on the Mount to something totally different or distorted the details of Jesus' death and resurrection? In other words, if you had an incomplete version of the message God wanted you to have or had a distorted picture of Jesus, it could very well impact you this way:

_____

_____

_____

Read Deuteronomy 11:26-28. Obeying God's instructions is for your protection and provision. If you were to identify at least one of God's commands from Scripture and describe how obedience provides some benefit or blessing and how it protects you from harm, it would be this command:

_____

_____

It's amazing when you think that God's Word comes directly from his heart's desire that you know him intimately. He wants you to know of his desire to provide for you and protect you and he has revealed himself in Scripture. How does that realization change your view of the Bible?

_____

_____

The psalmist David said, "Happy are people of integrity, who follow the law of the LORD. Happy are those who obey his decrees and search for him with all their hearts" (Psalm 119:1-2).

Read Psalm 119:4-16 aloud, and make King David's words your own prayer to God. (If you are in a group, read it in unison.)

> *Teach me, O LORD,*
> *to follow every one of your*
> *principles.*
> *Give me understanding and I will*
> *obey your law;*
> *I will put it into practice with all my heart.*
> *—Psalm 119:33-34*

What do these verses say to you about your attitude toward God's Word? Express it to God. *"God, you have given me your reliable words and I want to…"*

_____

_____

_____. *"*

|||||||||||||||||||||||||||||||||||||||||||||||||||||||||||||||||||||||||||||||||||||||||||||||||||||||||||||||||

Truth Encounter

Read Psalm 119:1-2.

Reflect on Psalm 119:1-2 again. Now allow the Holy Spirit to help you recall a time when your choice to follow the teachings of the Bible brought blessings for your life. If possible, think of how you lived out a particular Bible verse and what blessing, or "happiness," resulted. To get you started, here are a few verses to consider:

- "If you give, you will receive" (Luke 6:38).
- "Give all your worries and cares to God, for he cares about what happens to you" (1 Peter 5:7).

- "Honor your father and mother. Then you will live a long, full life in the land the LORD your God will give you" (Exodus 20:12).
- "Trust in the LORD with all your heart; do not depend on your own understanding. Seek his will in all you do, and he will direct your paths" (Proverbs 3:5-6).
- "God blesses those who mourn, for they will be comforted" (Matthew 5:4).
- "If we confess our sins to him, he is faithful and just to forgive us and to cleanse us from every wrong" (1 John 1:9).

If you are in a group, share with one another how following God's ways brought blessing. It might sound like this:

"I remember a time when _____ and the biblical truth of

_____ proved to be a blessing. Following this truth brought happiness/blessing to my life by...

_____

_____."

(For example: "I remember a time when I was in college and the biblical truth of 1 Peter 5:7 proved to be a blessing. I gave my cares and worry about my audition to the Lord. I really felt a sense of peace because I knew that God cared for me, and I could go into my audition secure in his love. Following this truth brought happiness to my life because the director actually told me that I didn't appear nervous—and then I got the part!")

Truth Talk—An Assignment for the Week

"We loved you so much that we gave you not only God's Good News but our own lives, too" (1 Thessalonians 2:8-9).

Consider the following ideas and make plans to initiate a spiritual conversation this week with someone. Share an insight that you might have had in this session, and as you do, relationally share a part of yourself with another. If you have a child or teenager at home, make sure to prioritize a time to start these spiritual conversations with them. Consider saying something like one of these examples:

1 "I've been going through a study guide on truths of the faith. And I've been reminded how living out the truths of the Bible actually brings blessings or happiness to life. I've been especially grateful for the truth of…

_____

_____."

2 "I've been amazed at how 'doing' Bible verses can really work in my life. I 'did' a verse the other day when…

_____

_____."

("I spoke calmly to my angry son. I 'experienced' Proverbs 15:1 and saw my gentle answer turn away his hot anger"; or "I went to bed meditating on how I can cast my cares on the Lord. I 'experienced' 1 Peter 5:7 and now I'm sleeping better, relaxing better, and am even less irritable!")

3 "I have always thought of the Bible as only a set of rules and teachings, but now I'm beginning to see it as…

_____. I'm so grateful that God has

given us His Word because…

_____

_____."

Ask God to provide an opportunity for you to share one or more of these TruthTalks with a friend, co-worker, child, teen, family member, or someone who needs Christ.

Read chapters 12–15 of *The Unshakable Truth* book this week.

Close Your Time in Prayer

TRUTH THREE: ORIGINAL SIN

What Are We Talking About?

Would you say most people you know are pretty good people? There seem to be a lot of good people in life, and there are even a few saintly people. Then there are those who are not so good, and finally a few absolutely evil individuals.

When you were growing up did you think of yourself as being a good kid or a bad sort of kid?

"As a kid I would say I was…

_____

_____

_____

_____ ."

In your opinion, what qualifies a person as being good or bad?

"I consider a person good when he or she…

_____

_____

_____ ."

"I consider a person bad when he or she…

_____

_____

_____ ."

We are talking about Truth Three: Original Sin

Session Objective

To more clearly understand what causes wrong attitudes and actions and determine how to make right choices in life.

Video

Now play DVD Session Three, Part 1, or go back to **www.unshakable truth.com/sg** and click on "Video Menu" and then on "Session Three, Part 1" to view Josh and Sean introducing this truth for 5 minutes.

How Do You Answer?

Where does evil come from—from our environment and culture, or from within a person?

"I believe evil comes from…

_____

_____

because _____

_____."

Read Isaiah 64:6. Select the point of view below that you most agree with and complete the answer.

"I believe there is some good in every person and here's why:

_____

_____

_____."

Truth Three: Original Sin

We believe the truth that God created humans in his image to relate to him lovingly, but that relationship was destroyed because of original sin. Sin was passed to the entire human race, and consequently all are born spiritually dead and utterly helpless to gain favor with God.

"I believe we are all infected with sin and here's why:

_____

_____

_____. *"*

Video

Now play DVD Session Three, Part 2, or go back to **www.unshakable truth.com/sg** and click on "Video Menu" and then on "Session Three, Part 2" to view Josh and Sean discussing this truth for 11 minutes.

How It Applies

Sean said, "When we understand the nature of our own sinfulness we must then learn to make right choices." And there is a definite process we can learn so we can make right choices every time, as described in the following portion of chapter 14 of *The Unshakable Truth* book.

"Even after we become Christians—Christ followers—we must learn how to make right, godly choices.

"God and God alone is the arbiter of what is right and what is wrong. He is the absolute standard of rightness, and everything moral flows from his innate nature. When anyone decides that they alone know what is right for them, they are in effect worshipping the god of self. Right, godly choices that bring fulfillment and joy to our lives are those that relationally align with the person and character of a holy, righteous God. He and he alone establishes the boundaries of right and wrong—which, by the way, are always in our best interest.

"There is a relational process of making right moral choices that, if followed, will bring God's protection and provision in life every time. We have distilled this process

into an easy-to-remember formula that we call the '4-Cs.' Each time you and I are confronted with a moral choice we can follow the process to 1) Consider the Choice; 2) Compare the Choice to God; 3) Commit to God's Way; and 4) Count on God's Protection and Provision."

A Case Study in Honesty
"Your Loss Is My Gain"

How would you respond?

"You bought a fan at the local hardware store. The first time you plugged the device in and tried to turn it on, it would not work. You took the screw out of the casing, took the casing off, and looked inside to see if you could spot any problem in the wiring. You are not a mechanic and know little about electricity, so without touching any of the mechanisms or wiring you simply replace the casing. You take the fan back to the store and ask for a replacement or a refund.

"'I'm sorry,' the supervisor says. 'We just can't replace a fan that has been damaged this way. It is clear that this screw has been tampered with. That indicates internal tampering, which no doubt caused the electrical short.'

"'I'm telling you,' you persist, 'I didn't tamper with anything! It wouldn't work the first time I tried it.'

"'There is nothing more I can do,' the supervisor responds. 'We can repair the fan, but there will be a service charge.'

"'Forget it,' you angrily retort and storm out of the hardware store.

"A few weeks later, you are checking out at the same hardware store after purchasing $50 or so worth of various items. As you walk to your car you look at your receipt and recount the change the clerk gave you. The clerk has undercharged you by $10. What is your first impulse? Remember this is the same store that did you an injustice."

_____

_____

_____

Follow the process of the 4-C's.

- *Consider the choice.* It may be easy to simply disregard the clerical error and go on your way without another thought. Especially since the clerk's error would seem to balance the cheating you had suffered earlier from the same store. But there is a choice to be made here, and it is important for you to pause and consider the choice. Either you can a) go back inside and return the $10 you received in error, or b) keep them as partial repayment for the money you lost when the store cheated you. What are you inclined to do?

  _____

  _____

  _____

- *Compare it to God.* Your natural impulse may be to keep the money. But you need to stop and think how that choice compares with God's character. Ask yourself, *If this store had cheated Jesus and then later had accidentally given him too much change, what would he have done?*

  Read 1 Peter 2:22-23. What did Jesus do specifically when he was wrongly persecuted?

  _____

  _____

  _____

- *Commit to God's ways.* You have a decision to make, but you have a problem. Under ordinary circumstances you would return the money, but you figure your present situation is a special case. The hardware store has "cheated" you out of the cost of a fan repair. So really, keeping the $10 mistake helps to settle the score. So are you justified in keeping the extra money? Why or why not?

  Before you answer, read *Leviticus 19:13* and *1 Peter 3:9 and 17.*

  _____

  _____

  _____

- *Count on God's protection and provision.* What would you gain if you justified keeping the money?

_____

_____

What do you gain by returning the money? *Read Psalm 15:1,4-5. "I gain…*

_____

_____."

Read Proverbs 22:1. "I gain…

_____

_____."

Read Psalm 34:12-14. "I gain…

_____

_____."

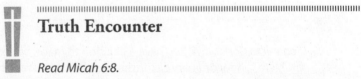

Truth Encounter

Read Micah 6:8.

Reflect on the importance of right choices, in contrast to our natural inclinations. Recall a time when you faced some kind of "moral dilemma" (like the hardware store example) and—whether you realized it or not—you lived out the 4-Cs and made choices pleasing to God. Perhaps your right choices involved money or telling the truth. You might have made a right choice to admit you were wrong or make things right with another person.

Complete these thoughts, and if you're in a group take turns sharing these with the others.

"I remember the time when (describe the situation)…

_____

_____

_____ *."*

"I could have chosen to (describe the natural or sinful choice that could have been made)…

_____

_____

_____ *."*

"But my choice led instead to (describe the right choice you did make)…

_____

_____

_____ *."*

(For example: "I remember the time I was tempted to take some shoes that were left at a camp retreat. I remember thinking, *That kid's parents have so much money, they can just buy some more.* Nobody would have known, since they had obviously been forgotten, but I was led instead to turn in the shoes to the camp office. I was so grateful I had done so because I later found out that the shoes actually belonged to a kid who really needed them.")

As you share these recollections with your group, rejoice together over the right choices that were a blessing to both God and others! "When others are happy, be happy with them" (Romans 12:15a). Celebrate together the Spirit's work that empowered you to live out God's Word.

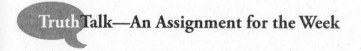 Truth Talk—An Assignment for the Week

Make plans to initiate a conversation this week with someone. If you have a child or teenager at home, make sure to prioritize a time to start these conversations with them. Consider saying something like:

33

1 "I've been going through a study and learning how our relationship with God and others gets broken by our sin. I've been remembering some times when I made some godly choices and other times when I haven't. I've realized I can count on God's provision and protection in the midst of hard choices because…

_____

_____."

2 "God has been showing me some of the ways I have failed to make godly choices. I want to apologize to you for my

_____. I was wrong to

_____

and I have asked God to forgive me. Will you forgive me?"

3 "I've been thinking about how my own choices impact my relationship with God and with others. I can see how my faith in Jesus has made a difference in the choices I make. I'm so glad that a relationship with him has changed me by…

_____

_____."

Read chapters 16–19 of *The Unshakable Truth* book this week.

Close Your Time in Prayer

TRUTH FOUR: GOD BECAME HUMAN

What Are We Talking About?

What does God do about broken relationships? Read the following from chapter 16 of *The Unshakable Truth* book:

"*In the beginning Adam and Eve experienced a wonderful love relationship with God in the perfect Garden of Eden. There was no hunger, greed, fear, or pain because God's holy presence produced nothing but goodness. But after they sinned, they were banished from the garden.*

"They were no longer innocent—instead they were guilty. They no longer delighted in God—instead they felt fear and shame. Rather than basking in God's favor and enjoying his provisions, they worked the cursed ground and sweated to make ends meet. Their sin had left them feeling alone and unacceptable.

"But how did God feel? Was he angry and vindictive? Did he never again want anything to do with the human creation that had rebelled against him?"

How do you tend to feel and what do you do when one of your children or close friends does something against you—like lie about you, talk behind your back, and make fun of you?

"It makes me feel _____.

And I tend to _____. *"*

Continue:

"How did God feel? Instead of anger, God felt grief and sadness. From one generation after another his cherished humans lived a life of sin and rebellion and 'it broke his heart'" (Genesis 6:6).

"So what did God do? He took the initiative. We are the ones who desperately need him, but we didn't seek him out. We are the ones who should have been crying out for help. Yet the all-sufficient Lord, who 'has no needs…[but] gives life and breath to everything, and…satisfies every need there is' wants you and wants me (Acts 17:25). We rejected him yet he still accepted us. He wants to relate to us—to enjoy and delight and take pleasure in a personal relationship with us. He wants to complete our joy.

"So God entered our world to cancel the curse of sin and death that has power over us. He 'became human and lived here on earth among us' (John 1:14). 'Because God's children are human beings—made of flesh and blood—Jesus also became flesh and blood by being born in human form. For only as a human being could he die, and only by dying could he break the power of the Devil, who had the power of death' (Hebrews 2:14). 'God's secret plan has now been revealed to us; it is a plan centered on Christ' (Ephesians 1:9). Only the Son of the living God could wrench the power of death out of the hand of our archenemy, Satan, so God could be reconnected to his children in a personal, one-on-one relationship."

We are talking about Truth Four: God Became Human

Session Objective

To come to a greater understanding of how God's entering our world lets us know he understands us completely.

🎬 Video

Now play DVD Session Four, Part 1, or go back to **www.unshakable truth.com/sg** and click on "Video Menu" and then on "Session Four, Part 1" to view Josh and Sean introducing this truth for 5 minutes.

Truth Four: God Became Human

We believe the truth of the incarnation (God becoming human), in which God accepted us without condition and sent Jesus Christ, born of the Virgin Mary, to redeem us and restore us to a relationship with him.

How Do You Answer?

Do you believe Jesus is the Son of God who came to save us?

"Yes, I believe Jesus is the one sent to save us because…

_____
_____
_____."

"I have doubts or can't explain why I believe Jesus is sent to save us because…

_____
_____
_____."

When it really comes down to it, does it matter if Jesus was God in human form? Isn't it his teachings that are the important thing? If you agree it doesn't matter if Jesus is God's Son, and it's really all about his teachings, then why is that the case?

_____
_____
_____

Or, if you think it's very important that Jesus is God's Son, then why?

_____
_____
_____

Video

Now play DVD Session Four, Part 2, or go back to **www.unshakabletruth .com/sg** and click on "Video Menu" and then on "Session Four, Part 2" to view Josh and Sean discussing this truth for 12 minutes.

||||||||||||||||||||||||||||||||||||||||||||||||||||||||||||||||||||||||||||||||||||||||||||||||||||||||||||||

How It Applies

Jesus' claim to be God (Deity) leaves us with two alternatives: Either his claim is true or it is false. And if his claim is false we are left with two added options (see diagram).

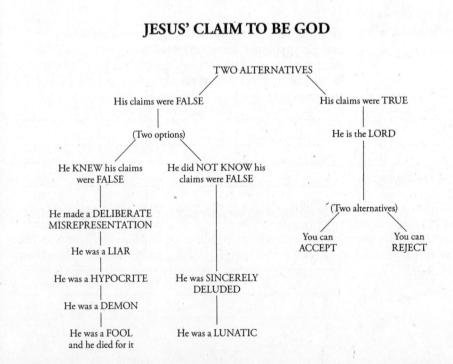

JESUS' CLAIM TO BE GOD

How does this give you greater confidence that Jesus is who he claimed to be? In other words,

"When I think of the alternatives in Jesus' claim to Deity, it...

_____

_____

_____."

Jesus Came to Redeem You

God sent his Son to earth in human form to redeem you. Do you tend to feel you deserve being redeemed—just a little?

"Yes, I think I'm deserving of God's mercy because...

_____

_____

_____."

Or, *"I don't think I'm deserving of God's mercy because...*

_____

_____

_____."

Read Romans 5:6-8.

"God in all his fullness was pleased to live in Christ, and by him God reconciled everything to himself. He made peace with everything in heaven and on earth by means of his blood on the cross. This includes you who were once so far away from God. You were his enemies, separated from him by your evil thoughts and actions" (Colossians 1:19-21).

Think for a moment of your most shameful acts and wrong attitudes. Despite all of them God accepts you so much he died for you. How does that make you feel?

_____

_____

What do you think it is about God that enables him to accept you like that?

_____

_____

God Knows You Intimately and Understands You Completely

God entered our world and took on human form and that lets us know he understands what we are going through. Take a moment and describe some experiences you have gone through.

Have you experienced rejection? If you have, describe it: "I felt rejected when…

_____

_____

_____."

Have you experienced abandonment? If you have, describe it: "I felt a sense of abandonment when…

_____

_____

_____."

Have you experienced someone misunderstanding you? If you have, describe it: "I felt misunderstood when…

_____

_____

_____."

Have you experienced ridicule? If you have, describe it: "I felt ridiculed when…

_____

_____

_____."

Have you experienced betrayal or criticism? If you have, describe it: "I felt criticized or betrayed when…

_____

_____

_____."

Is it sometimes hard to sense that the Lord of the universe identifies with you when you suffer such things? Consider the following from chapter 18 of *The Unshakable Truth* book:

"Think of it: Jesus is the all-sufficient Lord, yet when he was born to Mary he became as dependent as you were when you were a baby. He was the one who fashioned the human body, yet like you he had to learn to walk. He was the preexistent Word, yet he had to learn to speak, just as you did. He created clouds and rivers and lakes, yet he got thirsty. He endured the taunts of those who knew only part of his family's story. He must have felt the almost unbearable weight of grief when his earthly father, Joseph, died. He suffered not only the physical torture of the cross as he died for you but also the anguish of being rejected, humiliated, denied, abandoned, and even betrayed by his closest friends. Why did he willingly go through all that?

"Because he wants you to know that he understands. He suffered like a human being, and he wants to affirm you in your suffering. The writer of Hebrews tells us that Christ 'has gone through suffering and temptation…[and] is able to help us when we are being tempted…[He] understands our weaknesses, for he faced all of the same temptations we do, yet he did not sin. So let us come boldly…and we will find grace to help us when we need it' (Hebrews 2:18; 4:15-16). There is nothing you have experienced that God in Christ does not understand firsthand! He, like you, has experienced

- *rejection—by his own people,*
- *abandonment—by his own disciples,*
- *misunderstanding—by his own followers,*
- *ridicule—at his own trial,*

- *betrayal—by a close friend, and*
- *criticism—by the religious leaders of his day."*

Truth Encounter

Read Romans 12:15b.

Jesus experienced sorrow, and he understands what you are going through no matter what it involves. Pause quietly and allow the Holy Spirit to help you think of a time recently or in the past when you experienced some measure of sorrow. Perhaps it is an experience you have already written down. If you are in a group, share that experience with the others.

"I recall being (rejected, abandoned, misunderstood, ridiculed, betrayed, criticized, or something else) when…

_____

_____

_____."

As each person shares their time of sorrow, be certain that a few others in the group offer words of comfort. In obedience to Romans 12:15, when others are sad, "share their sorrow." Gather around the one in need and comfort him or her right now with words like "I am so sorry you are experiencing that" or "I hurt for you," and allow those words and sincere feelings to reflect Jesus' words of comfort and compassionate love. For those of you facing a difficulty or trial, receive the comfort and compassion coming from Jesus through your friends.

If you are going through this study apart from a group, allow the Holy Spirit to comfort you. Know that Jesus understands what you have or are now going through and he sorrows with you.

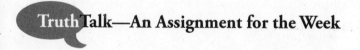

Truth Talk—An Assignment for the Week

For a devotional time with God this week, read Matthew 26:36-44. Identify with what Jesus must have felt when his closest friends couldn't stay awake and pray with him. Then allow God to encourage and comfort you. He knows the disappointments you experience in your life and promises to go through them with you. And remember that God "comforts us in all our troubles so that we can comfort others. When others are troubled, we will be able to give them the same comfort God has given us" (2 Corinthians 1:4). Be an instrument of God's comfort to someone this week and identify with their trial and difficulty. Following are three suggested TruthTalks.

1 "I've been going through a study and I've been learning how Jesus was not only God's Son, he was also completely human. That means Jesus experienced all the hurts that we've experienced. I've been especially comforted by the truth that Jesus knows what it's like to feel…

_____ because _____

_____

_____ ."

2 "I've recently had the opportunity to receive comfort from some of my friends and to have other people share in my sorrow; it was amazing to have others listen and care for me. Could I do that for you now?"

3 "I've recently had the privilege of 'doing' a Bible verse: Romans 12:15. It was amazing to mourn or share in the sorrows of one another. I feel so close to the people that shared that time with me. Romans 12:15 is such a simple verse, but I felt so blessed that…

_____

_____ ."

Ask God to provide an opportunity for you to share one or more of these TruthTalks with a friend, co-worker, child, teen, family member, or someone who needs Christ.

Read chapters 20–23 of *The Unshakable Truth* book this week.

Close Your Time in Prayer

TRUTH FIVE: CHRIST'S ATONEMENT FOR SIN

What Are We Talking About?

This story from chapter 20 of *The Unshakable Truth* book begins our discussion of the basis of forgiveness:

"I (Sean) grew up in the small mountain town of Julian, California. Most of my shopping was done at the general store in town. That is where I got candy, school supplies, crafts, and so on. My parents had dropped me, two of my school friends, and Katie, my five-year-old sister, off to do some shopping while they sat in the car. When we came out of the store, Katie had a handful of lapel pins and colorful craft pencils. As we walked to the car she handed them to my two friends and said, 'Here, I bought these things for you.'

"We got in the car, and Josh and Dottie looked at each other in a strange way. Dottie then got out and asked Katie to join her. My parents had sensed something was up because they hadn't given Katie any money to buy things. Within minutes I found out that my sister was a shoplifter!

"My dad and mom conferred with each other for a moment. Then Dottie collected the stolen goods, took her little thief by the hand, and walked her right back into the store.

"There are laws against shoplifting in California. Stealing is punishable by fines and jail time. Of course, I wasn't too worried. I figured with Katie returning the stolen stash and giving an apology, she'd be forgiven and go free.

"But what if the store owner had really been ticked at Katie? What if he refused to forgive and pressed charges? I figured the courts would then demand justice of my sister, and she would face the consequences—jail time. And I would have a convict for a sister.

"Of course, that didn't happen. Forgiveness was offered to Katie and she was set free of the consequences of stealing."

As a child, what was the first offense—any attitude or action—in which you remember needing forgiveness?

_____

_____

_____

Read Romans 3:20 and 23. Do you have a tendency to think that you can offset the things you've done wrong by doing more good deeds?

"Yes, I believe any wrong I do in God's eyes will be countered by the good things I do, because...

_____

_____

_____.*"*

"No, I don't believe God will somehow justify my bad deeds with my good ones, because...

_____

_____

_____.*"*

We are talking about Truth Five: Christ's Atonement for Sin.

Session Objective

To gain a deeper, heartfelt appreciation for what it took for God to forgive us of our sins.

Video

Now play DVD Session Five, Part 1, or go back to **www.unshakable truth.com/sg** and click on "Video Menu" and then on "Session Five, Part 1" to view Josh and Sean introducing this truth for 2 minutes.

How Do You Answer?

How important is it to you that people forgive you for blowing it?

"I want people to forgive me because…

_____

_____

_____ *."*

The idea of forgiveness is to set a person free of the offense against you, and that always comes at a cost. Think of a time someone wronged you. Explain the cost physically, emotionally, psychologically, financially, and so on, that was required of you to forgive that person. What sacrifice did you have to make to forgive?

_____

_____

_____

Video

Now play DVD Session Five, Part 2, or go back to **www.unshakable truth.com/sg** and click on "Video Menu" and then on "Session Five, Part 2" to view Josh and Sean discussing this truth for 14 minutes.

Truth Five: Christ's Atonement for Sin

We believe the truth that Jesus, as the sinless Son of God, atoned for our sin through his death on the cross. And the offering of his blood as a sacrifice for sin redeems us so we are forgiven—set free—and raises us to new life in him.

How It Applies

When we are confident in who Jesus is—the perfect Lamb of God—we can have confidence that we can be forgiven before God, as explained in chapter 21 of *The Unshakable Truth* book:

"When you are put on the justice scales of God, there is only one thing that can outweigh your sin. It isn't your good deeds, a life of penance, or even the sacrifice of your own life. The only thing that will cancel out your sin and satisfy the justice scales of a holy God is a pure and holy sacrifice.

"God told the children of Israel, 'I, the LORD your God, am holy' (Leviticus 19:2). And he made it clear that the sacrificial offerings to him had to be pure and without defects, offered up to him by holy priests. When these conditions were met he would accept the offering as a substitute for their sin and his justice scales were satisfied.

"The book of Hebrews tells us that not only did Jesus die for us, but he 'is the kind of high priest we need because he is holy and blameless, unstained by sin…He does not need to offer sacrifices every day like the other high priests…Jesus did this once for all when he sacrificed himself on the cross…[God's] Son has been made perfect forever' (Hebrews 7:26-28).

"If the Jesus of history born in Bethlehem some 2000 years ago was truly God's Son, then it is clear that he was the perfect

sacrifice and holy high priest needed to secure our salvation. And God wants us to feel confident in our faith that Jesus of Nazareth is the holy Lamb of God. That is why he has given us such clear signs."

What convinces you that the historical Jesus of Nazareth was in fact the "Lamb of God who takes away the sin of the world" (John 1:29)? Is it your faith in what you have been taught, your personal experience with God, the evidence Josh shared, or what?

_____

_____

_____

(If you would like more evidence that Jesus is God, see chapters 17, 21, and 25 of *The Unshakable Truth* book.)

God in the person of Jesus gave up so much for you to be forgiven. Identify some of what Jesus as God had to give up to redeem you. "Jesus gave up...

_____

_____

_____."

Jesus not only gave up so much to redeem you—he also had to endure and sacrifice so much for you to be forgiven. What are some of the emotional and relational things Jesus had to endure to purchase your salvation?

_____

_____

_____

What are some of the physical sacrifices Jesus made to enable you to be forgiven by God?

_____

_____

_____

Truth Encounter

Follow the instructions below.

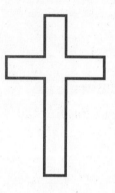

"Take a moment to look over the list above of what Jesus went through for you. Now stop and think of the sins you are most ashamed of—perhaps some you have never confessed to anyone except God. Identify past sins clearly in your mind (do not share them with your group) and then place a large solid dot ● within the cross to the left for each that comes to mind. Think of at least four to six of your shameful sins that needed God's forgiveness."

Now look at each of those dots carefully and then read the following. If you are in a group, have someone read this aloud.

"The cross fell into the hole with a loud thud that sent shock waves of pain through Jesus' legs and arms. Prior to being nailed to the cross he had been beaten almost beyond recognition. His closest friends had betrayed him, denied him, and abandoned him. Now he hung alone on the tree in excruciating pain. Soldiers below him gambled for his clothes. Religious leaders mocked him. He pressed his nail-pierced feet against the rough-hewn cross in attempts to get deep breaths. Each time he did this, pain shot up his legs. But he finally managed to draw enough breath to speak: 'Father, forgive these people… ' (Luke 23:34)

"Even though you have rejected him in the past, went your own way, and your sins are what nailed him to the cross—he loved you enough to sacrifice himself so you could be forgiven.

"He loved you so much that he sacrificed everything to remove the sin that separated you from God. Right now, fill in the cross with your pen or pencil blotting out all recognition of the dots that represent your sins. Scripture says, 'Oh, what joy for those whose disobedience is forgiven, whose sins are put out of sight. Yes, what joy for those whose sin is no longer counted against them by the Lord' (Romans 4:6-8)."

Take some time now and allow the Holy Spirit to lead you in a meditation upon Jesus at Calvary.

Jesus is bruised and beaten. Despised and rejected. He is soon to take on the sins of the world. This One who has never known sin is about to become sin—yours and mine. Why did he do it? Why was Christ willing to take on my sin? The answer is simple, but profound: *love.* The Sovereign Creator—who is free to live out his will any way he pleases—has chosen to give his own life!

Let's keep going. Who did he do this for? Meditate on the powerful answer: He did it for you!

If no one else had needed a Savior, God the Father would have allowed his Son to die, just for you.

Consider the wonder and gratitude of this truth: He did it for me!

Say it quietly in your heart and then write about it. "He did it for me!"

"Lord Jesus, as I reflect on your death and the sobering words 'You did it for me,' my heart is touched with…

_____

_____

_____."

Take time to pray the sentence prayers above aloud with your small group.

Conclude your prayers with, "Now there is no condemnation for those who belong to Christ Jesus. For the power of the life-giving Spirit has freed you through Christ Jesus from the power of sin that leads to death" (Romans 8:1-2).

Truth Talk—An Assignment for the Week

Jesus said, "Just as I have loved you, you should love each other" (John 13:34). The apostle John said, "We know what real love is because Christ gave up his life for us. And so we ought to give up our lives for our Christian brothers and sisters" (1 John 3:16). "Give up your life" this week in some form of sacrifice of your time and energy to meet another person's need. Specifically ask God to help you love someone sacrificially, as he has loved you. See the following TruthTalk suggestions.

1 "During a study I've been going through, I was overwhelmed with gratitude because of this truth: If no one else had needed Christ's death on the cross, he would have given his life just for me. That truth is amazing to me because…

_____

_____."

2 "I've had many sleepless, guilt-ridden nights because of how my sinful choices have impacted my life and the lives of others. This week, though, I experienced some relief because I embraced the truth that Jesus 'took' my sins upon himself. I am so grateful for God's provision for me and his forgiveness because…

_____

_____."

3 "I'm not very good at sacrificing myself for others, although I've found it less difficult to make sacrifices for other people in my life when I remember how Jesus has sacrificed himself for me. I've been grateful for His sacrifice of _____

_____ and that has empowered me to

_____

_____."

Read chapters 24–27 of *The Unshakable Truth* book this week.

Close Your Time in Prayer

TRUTH SIX: JUSTIFICATION THROUGH FAITH

What Are We Talking About?

Josh tells about the beginning of his transformation in these paragraphs from chapter 26 of *The Unshakable Truth* book:

"*When I (Josh) left home and headed off to college I was determined to find happiness. My quest for happiness took me through religion, education, and prestige, only to be disappointed at each turn. But God was faithful to me. I didn't love him, but he loved me. I could sense Jesus at the door of my heart pleading, 'Look, I have been standing at your door and constantly knocking. If you hear me calling and will open the door I will come in' (paraphrased from Revelation 3:20). I was in my second year at the university and I was keeping that door shut and bolted. I didn't care if Jesus did walk on water or turn water into wine. I didn't want any party pooper spoiling my fun. I couldn't think of any faster way to ruin my good times. I called them good times, but I was really miserable. I was a walking battlefield. My mind was telling me that Christianity was true, but my will was resisting it with all the energy it could muster.*

"*Then there was the pride problem. At that time the thought of becoming a Christian shattered my ego. I had just proved that all my previous thinking had been wrong and my friends had been right. Every time I got around those enthusiastic Christians, the inner conflict would boil over. If you've ever been in the company of happy people when you are miserable, you know how their joy can get under your skin. Sometimes I would literally get up, leave the group, and run right out of the student union. It came to the point where I would go to bed at ten o'clock at night but wouldn't get to sleep until four in the morning. I couldn't let go of the problem. I had to do something before it drove me out of my mind.*"

Josh became a follower of Christ despite his pride and skepticism. Perhaps you are a Christian as well. But what is it specifically that saved you and transformed your life into a child of God? Is it your acts of penance, some promises you made to God, your faith, or what?

_____

_____

_____

We are talking about Truth Six: Justification Through Faith

Session Objective

To more clearly understand how we are justified before God, and to follow the steps of becoming justified before God if that has never taken place in our life.

 Video

Now play DVD Session Six, Part 1, or go back to **www.unshakabletruth .com/sg** and click on "Video Menu" and then on "Session Six, Part 1" to view Josh and Sean introducing this truth for 3 minutes.

How Do You Answer?

In the interviews, people said that faith saves us. Does our faith actually justify us before God?

"Yes, I believe my faith actually justifies me before God because...

_____

_____

_____."

"No, I don't believe faith itself justifies me before God because…

_____

_____

_____ *."*

Read Ephesians 2:8. What does Scripture say you are saved by? _____
Then if you are saved by the merciful and loving grace of God that you don't
merit, what does your faith do?

_____

_____

_____

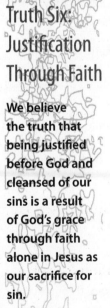

Truth Six: Justification Through Faith

We believe the truth that being justified before God and cleansed of our sins is a result of God's grace through faith alone in Jesus as our sacrifice for sin.

Video

Now play DVD Session Six, Part 2, or go back to **www.unshakabletruth.com/sg** and click on "Video Menu" and then on "Session Six, Part 2" to view Josh and Sean discussing this truth for 13 minutes.

How It Applies

A relationship with God is possible by his grace through our faith in Jesus, as this excerpt from chapter 24 of *The Unshakable Truth* book explains:

"Our righteousness before God is made possible through our faith in Jesus. Faith is the arm that reaches out to receive God's grace. And it is Christ who solves our sin problem past, present, and future. Because of Christ's atoning death, we too can claim the promise God made to Israel: 'No matter how deep the stain of your sins, I can remove it. I can make you as clean as freshly

fallen snow. Even if you are stained as red as crimson, I can make you as white as wool' (Isaiah 1:18).

"So is there nothing we can say to God or do for God that would merit our redemption? Is there nothing we can do to earn our justification? Is there nothing we can leverage to live right before God? Paul asked and answered those questions when he wrote, 'Can we boast then, that we have done anything to be accepted by God? No, because our acquittal is not based on our good deeds. It is based on our faith [in Jesus]. So we are made right with God through faith and not by obeying the law' (Romans 3:27-28).

"Performance-based people who want to earn what they get may find salvation by grace through faith hard to grasp, or at least hard to accept. But there is no human requirement to obtain God's offer of a relationship except to freely accept it. It is a gift based upon the requirements fulfilled by Jesus. That is why when speaking of salvation Paul said, 'It does not depend on the man who wills or the man who runs, but on God who has mercy' (Romans 9:16 NASB).

"Christ atoned for our sin by his death on the cross. When we place our faith in him as our substitute, we are redeemed and justified before God. We are set apart as his holy people. Not by what we have done, but because of what Christ has done. 'Abraham believed God, and God counted him as righteous because of his faith. When people work, their wages are not a gift, but something they have earned. But people are counted as righteous not because of their work, but because of their faith in God who forgives sinners' (Romans 4:3-4 NLT)."

Based on what you have heard from Josh and Sean and from these Scripture passages, think about this question again: "What specifically saved you and transformed your life into a child of God?" Is your answer any different than before? If so, in what way is it different now?

_____

_____

_____

When did you become justified before God as a result of his grace through your faith in Jesus?

"I was _____ years old when I trusted in Christ to redeem me."

"The circumstance surrounding my commitment was (write out what took place)

_____

_____

_____. "

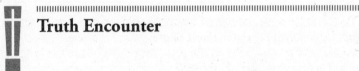

Truth Encounter

If you have never made a clear commitment to trust in Christ or you are unsure of your standing with God, today can be a new beginning. If you are in a group, walk through the following together. As an individual, answer the following questions and allow the Holy Spirit to guide you into a relationship with God.

Jesus said, "If any of you wants to be my follower, you must put aside your selfish ambition, shoulder your cross daily, and follow me. If you try to keep your life for yourself, you will lose it. But if you give up your life for me, you will find true life" (Luke 9:23-25).

- Do you recognize you have a problem with God? _____
  Do you admit you have sinned against God and gone your own way?

  _____

- Do you realize Jesus is your only hope and solution to your separation (death) from God because of sin? _____

  Read Romans 3:21-26.

- Will you respond to Christ as he says to you now, "I am the resurrection and the life. Those who believe in me, even though they die like everyone else, will live again. They are given eternal life for believing in me and will never perish" (John 11:25-26)? _____

  Tell God: "I have sinned against you and gone my own way. I ask you to forgive me. Right now I am turning away from my old life and placing my trust in Jesus Christ as my atoning sacrifice for sin. Raise me from death—my separation from you—to a new life of eternal relationship with you."

- Thank Jesus for transforming you from death to life.

  Say, "Thank you, Jesus, for making me a forgiven child of God and bringing me into a relationship with your Father—and now my Father God. Amen."

Read Romans 6:5-11. If you are in a group, explain what this passage means to you and your future life in Christ. Otherwise, write it out here.

_____

_____

_____

Truth Talk—An Assignment for the Week

If you have just trusted in Christ as your Savior, read John chapter 3 three times this week and tell at least three other people of the important decision you made today. For those who are already followers of Christ, share your testimony with three other people this week. See the suggestions below.

1 "As I was going through a study on justification by grace I was overwhelmed with gratitude. I was overwhelmed by all that I have received because of God's grace. Because of God's incredible grace (which is his undeserved favor and love), I have/am…

_____ ."

I was particularly grateful for this truth because…

_____

_____ ."

2 "I've been more amazed by God's grace lately because…

_____

_____ ."

3 "I 'get' what it means to have 'faith in Jesus,' because I am so grateful that God has...

_____

_____ . "

Read chapters 28–31 of *The Unshakable Truth* book this week.

||||||||||||||||||||||||||||||||||||||||||||||||||||||||||||||||||||||||||||||||||||||||||||||||||||||||||||||||

Close Your Time in Prayer

Truth Seven: Living the Transformed Life

What Are We Talking About?

What is transformation in the Christian life? This story from chapter 28 of *The Unshakable Truth* book starts to answer the question.

"*Carl is hungry all the time. He is obsessed with eating. He thinks of nothing except keeping his stomach full. You see, Carl is a caterpillar, and as a caterpillar he will shed his skin four or five times in order to make room for the steady supply of leaves his insatiable appetite demands. In fact, he will increase his weight ten-thousand-fold in less than 20 days. His gluttonous appetite will cause tremendous damage to crops and the economy of humans. There is nothing of lasting value or worth to say about Carl the caterpillar.*

"*But something marvelous is about to happen to Carl. Deep inside something calls him to stop eating and yield to a process of being fully encapsulated by a mysterious substance that hardens around him.*

"*Many days pass, and then it happens. Carl bursts out of his cocoon. He has undergone a radical change called metamorphosis. He is now a new creature with new habits and a whole new look...because Carl the caterpillar, obsessed only with fulfilling his gluttonous appetite, has been transformed into a beautiful butterfly. He no longer crawls about with a ravenous appetite that destroys crops. He now soars through the air, flying from plant to plant, pollinating flowers to enhance the beauty of his world.*

"'*Those who live only to satisfy their own sinful desires,' Paul the apostle says, 'will harvest the consequences of decay and death' (Galatians 6:8). Like Carl the caterpillar, 'their god is their appetite, they brag about shameful things, and all they think about is this life here on earth' (Philippians 3:19).*

"*But deep within our souls a voice is heard. It is the voice of God that calls us out of sin and death so a miraculous metamorphosis can take place. For 'those who become Christians become new persons. They are not the same anymore, for the old life is gone. A new life has begun! All this newness of life is from God, who brought us back to himself through what Christ did' (2 Corinthians 5:17-18)."*

The majority of people in the United States say they are Christians. Yet studies reveal that the lives of the majority of these professed Christians are rather un-Christlike, and essentially no different than non-Christians. Why do you think that is the case?

"Today, I think people who profess to be Christians don't live up to the name be-cause…

_____

_____

_____*."*

What specific changes did you experience in your life when you became a fol-lower of Jesus? Were they sudden changes or gradual ones?

"When I became a Christian my life changed this way:

_____

_____

_____*."*

||||||||||||||||||||||||||||||||||||||||||||||||||||||||||||||||||||||||||||||||||||||||||||||||||||||||||||||||

Session Objective

To more clearly define our purpose in life—why each of us is here.

Video

Now play DVD Session Seven, Part 1, or go back to **www.unshakable truth.com/sg** and click on "Video Menu" and then on "Session Seven, Part 1" to view Josh and Sean intro-ducing this truth for 2 minutes.

We are talking about Truth Seven: Living the Transformed Life

How Do You Answer?

You have certain talents and gifts that may identify what you do best in life, but for what basic reason did God create you—that is, from God's perspective what is your essential purpose for living?

"If I were to crystallize what I think God's purpose for me is, it would be…

_____

_____

_____

_____."*

In whose image and likeness were we created? (Read Genesis 1:26.) _____

As sons of Adam and daughters of Eve, do we naturally do a good job of reflecting God's likeness and image?

"I think I do a pretty good job of reflecting a godly image in my life because…

_____

_____

_____."*

Or, *"I think I struggle to reflect a godly image in my life because…*

_____

_____

_____."*

Do some scriptural research. Read Romans 8:29; Ephesians 4:23; and 2 Corinthians 3:18.

Based on these passages, what would you say your purpose is—why are you here? Is it different from your previous answer? How?

"I would say my purpose is…

_____

_____

_____.*"*

Why Are We Here?

"Our purpose in life is to honor our Creator God by living in relationship with him and out of that relationship become more and more like him. God created us to bring glory to himself. And we glorify God—reflect honorably upon him—as we love him and live devotedly committed to him, desiring to please him. 'Whatever you eat or drink or whatever you do,' Paul said, 'you must do all for the glory of God' (1 Corinthians 10:31).

"You and I begin to fulfill our purpose when we begin to live out the Godlike life he designed for us. He created us to relate to him and enjoy all the blessings that come from being godly."

 Video

Now play DVD Session Seven, Part 2, or go back to **www.unshakable truth.com/sg** and click on "Video Menu" and then on "Session Seven, Part 2" to view Josh and Sean discussing this truth for 15 minutes.

Truth Seven: Living the Transformed Life

We believe the truth that followers of Christ are meant to live in relationship with God and be transformed into the likeness of Christ, which defines our very purpose for living—to honor and glorify God.

How It Applies

When God transforms us from the inside out we begin to think and act differently. But we often need to remind ourselves that God sees us as his child, as described in chapter 30 of *The Unshakable Truth*.

"Living a Christlike life in part is about discovering the new person we already are in relationship with Christ and acting accordingly. *It's about interacting with and relating to Christ so the grace and power of God's Spirit is appropriated within us. Studying the Bible, attending church, and sharing our faith do not cause God to regard us as more redeemed, justified, sanctified, or adopted as his child. He already sees us in these ways because they define who we really are. So we don't do our way into becoming God's adopted children; we don't do things to cause his divine nature to dwell within us. We are not changed from the outside in; we are changed from the inside out. As we live in relationship with Christ, we can start behaving according to our new nature and do those things that God's children do—act like Christ."*

The truest statements about your transformed relationship with God are what God says about you in his Word. It has been said that our self-concept and our actions are largely determined by what we believe the most important person in our lives thinks about us.

The first two chapters of Ephesians provide a concentrated look at your attributes as a new creation in Christ. Translate these attributes into the first person and fill in the blanks describing your relationship from God's point of view.

Read these verses from Ephesians:

1:3—I am _____.

1:4—I was _____

_____.

1:5—I was _____

_____.

1:7—I have _____

_____.

1:7—I am _____.

1:11—I have received _____

_____.

1:13—I am identified as _____

_____.

Now go on to Ephesians chapter 2.

2:5—I am _____.

2:6—I am seated _____

_____.

2:7—I am _____.

2:8—I am _____.

2:10—I am _____.

2:13—I belong _____.

2:18—I have _____

_____.

You have all these things in Christ, and that is how God sees you. What makes it difficult for you to see yourself as God sees you? Why is it sometimes hard to accept your acceptance in him?

"I think I struggle to see myself as God sees me because…

_____

_____

_____."

"One of the keys to a continued transformation in Christ is to acknowledge that something very good happened to you when you trusted Christ. In Paul's words, you have 'clothed yourselves with a brand-new nature that is continually being renewed as you learn more and more about Christ, who created this new nature within you' (Colossians 3:10).

"You are not primarily what your parents, spouse, or friends say you are, even though many of them may be Christians. You are not what your negative emotions or condemning feelings may say you are. And you are certainly not what the godless culture says you are. You are who God says you are—nothing more, nothing less. The more you review, recite, and internalize the verbal picture God paints of you in Scripture, the better positioned you are to grow like that picture."

Truth Encounter

Recall that it was "by faith" that we received Christ, as the Holy Spirit drew us to him. And it is the Spirit's prompting of faith that unlocks the fullness of who we are in Christ.

By faith we are to trust in Christ to live the transformed life, because

- Christ is still *patient* when we are not.
- Christ is still *forgiving* when we want revenge.
- Christ still *loves* even when we do not.
- Christ is still *giving*—when we want to withhold.
- Christ is still *compassionate*—when we are insensitive.

Take time now to consider the list of five qualities above. Which of them might describe a need in your life? Consider both the privilege and responsibility of living out "who you are in Christ"!

"By faith, I want to express more of Christ's _____ through my life. I especially want to express more _____ toward (name specific person) _____."

(For example: "By faith, I want to express more of Christ's compassion through my life. I especially want to express more compassion toward my in-laws. I need

God to sensitize my heart and help me be more caring and compassionate as we prepare for them to live with us.")

If you're in a group, vulnerably share your response with others.

TruthTalk—An Assignment for the Week

As a devotion read Ephesians chapters 1 and 2 and personalize each passage that reflects who you are in Christ. Thank God each day for who you are in him and act accordingly. Then take time to share with family and friends about what God is revealing to you. For example, something like the following:

1 "During a study I'm going through I was reminded of how God has changed me. Because of Jesus, I have become more/less _____. I used to be _____, but because of Christ, I am _____."

2 "I now see myself the way God sees me—nothing more and nothing less. I'm grateful and amazed that God sees me as _____. This truth is beginning to make a difference in my life by _____ _____."

3 "God has impressed me with my need to become more _____ in my relationship with you. I want to be more _____ _____ because I love you/care for you. I'm asking God to make these changes in me, and I'm trusting him to do it."

Read chapters 32–35 of *The Unshakable Truth* book this week.

|||||||||||||||||||||||||||||||||||||||||||||||||||||||||||||||||||||||||||||||||||||||||||||

Close Your Time in Prayer

TRUTH EIGHT: JESUS' BODILY RESURRECTION

What Are We Talking About?

The importance of Jesus' teachings gains some perspective in this story from chapter 32 of *The Unshakable Truth* book.

" *S*he stood a few feet away sobbing as her son hung there, nailed to a rugged cross. John stood beside Mary, trying to comfort her. Moments later Jesus took one last breath and said, '"It is finished!" Then he bowed his head and gave up his spirit' (John 19:30).

"Joseph of Arimathea and a few women lowered Jesus' lifeless body from the cross and prepared him for burial. After placing their dead Messiah in the tomb, they rolled the large stone over the entrance to seal him away for good, or so many thought.

"Imagine a conversation between two observers of Jesus' ministry immediately after his death.

"'I thought this Messiah Movement was going to last,' Hamon says dryly.

"'Yeah, me too,' agrees Benjamin. 'I wonder what his disciples are going to do now?'

"'Oh, I think it'll be difficult,' Hamon responds, 'but they can still keep things going.'

"'How?' Benjamin asks skeptically. 'Without their Messiah they don't have a message!'

"'Sure they do,' Hamon argues. 'Of course, since Jesus is dead he can't marshal an army to overthrow the Romans, but his disciples can still propagate all his great teachings.'

"The two men ponder for a moment. Finally Benjamin says thoughtfully, 'Yeah, *they've lost their charismatic speaker and miracle worker, but they still have a lot of solid teaching, especially if they'll key on his "love your neighbor as yourself" theme. That should keep things going. Maybe they'll be just fine.'"*

When you stop and consider who Jesus was, what he taught, and the fact that he gave his life to save you, are his teachings the most important thing?

"Yes, I think overall the most important thing about Christianity is Jesus' teachings because…

_____

_____

_____.*"*

"No, Jesus' teachings are important, but the most important thing about Christianity isn't a set of teachings because…

_____

_____

_____.*"*

||||||||||||||||||||||||||||||||||||||||||||||||||||||||||||||||||||||||||||||||||||||||||||||||||||||||||||||||||||||

Session Objective

To more clearly recognize the absolute necessity of Jesus' literal bodily resurrection to secure our eternal salvation.

Video

Now play DVD Session Eight, Part 1, or go back to **www.unshakable truth.com/sg** and click on "Video Menu" and then on "Session Eight, Part 1" to view Josh and Sean introducing this truth for 2 minutes.

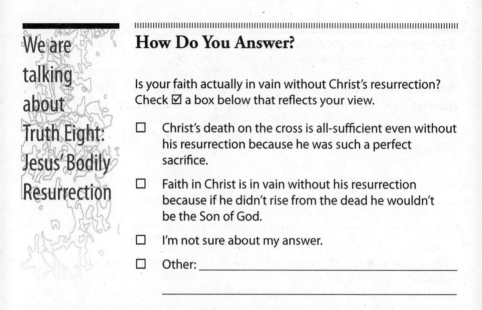

We are talking about Truth Eight: Jesus' Bodily Resurrection

How Do You Answer?

Is your faith actually in vain without Christ's resurrection? Check ☑ a box below that reflects your view.

☐ Christ's death on the cross is all-sufficient even without his resurrection because he was such a perfect sacrifice.

☐ Faith in Christ is in vain without his resurrection because if he didn't rise from the dead he wouldn't be the Son of God.

☐ I'm not sure about my answer.

☐ Other: _____

_____

Read Leviticus 16:15-19. Aaron, the high priest, went into the tabernacle's most holy place to sprinkle animal blood as a sacrifice on the altar. Who instructed Aaron and the children of Israel to build the tabernacle, the most holy place, and the altar, and to follow the rituals of the blood sacrifice? And what was their purpose?

"I would say the purpose of these specific instructions was to…

_____

_____

_____."

Read Hebrews 9:11-15,23-26.

Where is the temple/tabernacle in which this sacrifice was offered?

_____

Who was the High Priest who offered the sacrifice? _____

What was accomplished by this High Priest? _____

_____

Someone wrote a note that said,

"I cannot fully agree with you that our faith is in vain without Jesus' resurrection. Christ's sacrificial death is not meaningless without his resurrection. A sacrifice like that could never be meaningless."

Is it true that Jesus' sacrifice was not meaningless without his resurrection?

Based on Hebrews 9, what point is this person missing about the necessity of Jesus' resurrection?

_____

_____

_____

Christ's redemptive act wasn't just in dying. Christ's redemptive act was both in dying *and* in offering his own blood before God in his resurrected bodily form. He is the only perfect high priest qualified to present the holy sacrifice before God in the heavenly temple.

 Video

Now play DVD Session Eight, Part 2, or go back to **www.unshakable truth.com/sg** and click on "Video Menu" and then on "Session Eight, Part 2" to view Josh and Sean discussing this truth for 15 minutes.

Truth Eight: Jesus' Bodily Resurrection

We believe the truth that Jesus died on the cross as a sacrifice for our sins and on the third day rose bodily to life again in order to transform our lives and secure our eternal salvation.

How It Applies

Sean concluded by saying, "Isn't it wonderful that we can know that Jesus died and conquered the grave?" But to what end?

Read Romans 8:23-24.

Our belief in Christ's resurrection gives us hope and assurance of what?

_____

_____

_____

While Christ's resurrection offers us eternal life, our physical death is unavoidable and scary. Why is it so natural to fear death?

1. How much do you really know about death? Is the unknown aspect of this frightening to you? Why?

_____

_____

2. We don't die as a group—each person faces death on their own. Is this troubling to you? Why?

_____

_____

_____

3. Death robs us of the ones we love. Do you fear losing a loved one? _____

4. When we die, our goals die with us. How troubling is that to you? Explain.

_____

_____

_____

5. We don't know when death is coming, and we can't avoid it. Isn't that unavoidably a little scary? _____

Consider God's promises, as described in chapter 34 of *The Unshakable Truth* book.

"Yes, death is inevitable and so we all must die. But death isn't permanent for those who have trusted Christ. 'Everyone dies because all of us are related to Adam, the first man. But all who are related to Christ, the other man, will be given new life. But there is an order to this resurrection: Christ was raised first; then when Christ comes back, all his people will be raised' (1 Corinthians 15:22-23).

"Although we are redeemed, justified, sanctified, and adopted as God's children in this life, we have yet to gain the full rights of our adoption. Paul said that 'what we suffer now is nothing compared to the glory he will reveal to us later... for we long for our bodies to be released from sin and suffering. We, too, wait with eager hope for the day when God will give us our full rights as his adopted children, including the new bodies he has promised us. We were given this hope when we were saved' (Romans 8:18,23-24 NLT). That is the added relevance of Christ's resurrection. Not only are we forgiven of our sins and made right with God, but we also inherit a body that will live forever."

Truth Encounter

Because of Christ's resurrection and the promises he has made to us, our fear of death can be lifted. Because he lives...

- *The mystery of death is revealed.* Yes, death is mysterious and unknown, but after the resurrection of Jesus, we know something about it that we could not have known before. It is not permanent. Christ went through it, and he blazed a trail we can follow. Some of the mystery has been removed because we now have footprints to follow that we know will lead us into new life.

  Reflect on this realization and share with one another about this renewed sense of hope or write out your gratefulness to Jesus for breaking the power of death for us.

  _____

  _____

  _____

- *We don't have to face death alone.* Although from our perspective it may seem that we have to go through death alone, we now know this is an illusion. The death and resurrection of Jesus shows that this promise is not empty. Christ has actually stepped into the darkness of death and awaits us there with the light of life to lead us safely through.

  Reflect on this realization and share with one another about this renewed sense of hope, or write out how thankful you are that Jesus is with us in death.

  _____

  _____

  _____

- *We are not permanently separated from our loved ones.* The resurrection calms this fear as well. Because God has conquered death through Jesus Christ, our loving relationships will continue after death. Death may separate us temporarily from our loved ones, but the resurrection of Christ will bring us back together.

  Reflect on this realization and share the hope it gives you with those in your group, or write out how glad you are that Jesus is waiting for us on the other side of death.

  _____

  _____

  _____

- *Our personal hopes and dreams have a future.* The resurrection also does away with this fear. In fact, it would be accurate to say that in heaven all our hopes and dreams will be fulfilled.

  Reflect on this realization and share with the others what dreams you want fulfilled in heaven, or write those dreams out here.

  _____

  _____

  _____

- *Death is unavoidable, yet it is a transition to eternal life.* It's true that death is inevitable and no one can escape it. But because of Christ's resurrection, death is simply the passage to our eternal home in heaven.

  Reflect on this realization and share your heart of thanks with others for a resurrected Lord, or write out your thanks here.

  _____

  _____

  _____

Consider singing the Gaither song "Because He Lives."

Truth Talk—An Assignment for the Week

Scripture says, "Let heaven fill your thoughts. Do not think only about things down here on earth" (Colossians 3:2). This week as a devotional to God, spend time reading and meditating on Psalm 63:1-8 and 1 John 3:1-24. And then ask God to provide an opportunity for you to share one or more of the following with a friend, co-worker, young person, or family member.

1 "During a study this week, I was reminded of how Jesus conquered death—his resurrection shows us that even death is not permanent. Remembering Christ's resurrection has helped reassure me that...

_____

_____ ."

2 "When I think about the death of my friend/family member, I am definitely saddened by the loss. I am reassured though, that after this life, I will be with Jesus. That truth comforts my heart because...

_____

_____ ."

3 "I'm looking forward to a reunion in heaven with

_____ (name a particular person).
I can't wait to see them again. It's comforting to know that I
will be with them."

Read chapters 36–39 of *The Unshakable Truth* book this week.

||||||||||||||||||||||||||||||||||||||||||||||||||||||||||||||||||||||||||||||||||||||||||||||||||||||||||||||||||||

Close Your Time in Prayer

TRUTH NINE: THE TRINITY

What Are We Talking About?

Who are you as a person? Identify some of the roles or relationships you have that help define you. For example, you may be *a woman, a wife, a mother,* and so on.

"I am _____

_____

_____."

How many roles or relationships have you identified?

_____ Does this make you one person or multiple

people? _____

Or, are you one person with multiple roles? _____.

_____

Now, what about God? Is he one God with three different roles, or is he three different Gods with one purpose, or what?

_____

_____

_____

Read Matthew 3:13-17. In this passage the one true God is revealed for all to see and hear.

Who did John baptize? _____

Who descended like a dove upon Jesus? _____

Who spoke from heaven? _____

The three distinct persons of the Godhead, whom we call the Trinity, made their presence known in this passage.

Read Deuteronomy 6:4. What does it mean that the "Lord is one" (NIV), when we know that God exists as three persons?

_____

_____

_____

"While this illustration may be imperfect, it might be a helpful way to think about three in one. For example, the chemical combination H_2O can be a liquid (water), a solid (ice), or a gas (steam). Yet in each of these forms the chemical substance is one and the same. If you put an ice cube in a beaker and heat it, you will see a solid melting into liquid and then rising into a gas. As this operation is in process, you will have all three states of the H_2O chemical co-existing."

God is not one person with three different roles. Neither is he three Gods with one purpose. The Trinity is one God who eternally co-exists as three persons. The Father, Son, and Holy Spirit as three distinct persons share this one substance and essence of being God.

We are talking about Truth Nine: The Trinity

Since the Godhead has eternally existed as three persons, what one word describes God's existence that he has invited us to experience with him? _____

God didn't create humans because he needed a relationship; he already had relationship. He has eternally existed in relationship. The Father has always infinitely loved the Son. The Son has always infinitely loved the Father. The Holy Spirit has always infinitely loved both the Father and the Son. A continuous cycle of perfect relationships is ever being experienced within the Godhead. While we are unable to fully comprehend such a perfect and continuing relationship, all of us long to experience this kind of relationship ourselves.

Just as God is one in relationship by his very being, so he

created us to be one in relationship with him and one another. The oneness of the Trinity serves as more than our master model for such oneness. God's unity in the Trinity is the secret to unlocking how relationship is meant to work. While we can never comprehend God's oneness in relationship in an absolute sense, we can gain enough insight into this mystery to experience the true meaning of relationship. Uncovering the mystery of the Trinity is like peering into the very heart of God.

There are certain relational characteristics or qualities that exist within the Trinity.

What relational qualities exist between Jesus and his Father, based on John 5:19?

_____

_____

_____

What relational qualities exist between the Father and the Son, based on John 5:22?

_____

_____

_____

John 8:29 describes what kind of relationship between the Father and the Son?

_____

_____

_____

It is this infinite love in perfect relationship within the Trinity that produces a oneness beyond our comprehension. It is not a relationship in which power and authority are leveraged. It is not some hierarchical chain of command. It is a circle of relationships in which each person looks out for the best in the others because of their deep abiding love for one another. In their infinite love, the three persons of the Trinity are so intent on pleasing one another that the very essence of their beings is indistinguishable. Speaking in math terms, they are one to the infinite power.

In God we see three persons in perfect relationship and harmony because their nature is one. The Father so loved the world that he gave his Son. The Son so loved his Father that he gave his life. The Holy Spirit so loved the Father and the Son that he gave us himself (see Romans 5:5). And together they—one God—invite us into their love relationship.

The apostle Paul said, "May you experience the love of Christ, though it is so great you will never fully understand it" (Ephesians 3:19). We will "never fully understand it," perhaps because to comprehend God's love is to comprehend God—which is inconceivably beyond our human capacity. Yet the triune nature of God has been manifested to us. We see God's handiwork of creation made for us; he revealed himself in the flesh for our salvation; and we experience his empowering presence through his Spirit.

||||||||||||||||||||||||||||||||||||||||||||||||||||||||||||||||||||||||||||||||||||||||||||||||||||||||||||||||||

Session Objective

To discover how we can yield more to the Holy Spirit so we can experience the deeper meaning of relationship with the triune Godhead and live pleasing him.

Video

Now play DVD Session Nine, Part 1, or go back to **www.unshakable truth.com/sg** and click on "Video Menu" and then on "Session Nine, Part 1" to view Josh and Sean introducing this truth for 10 minutes.

Truth Nine: The Trinity

We believe the truth that there is one God who is eternally co-existing as the Father, Son, and Holy Spirit in a perfect relation-ship of oneness.

How Do You Answer?

Who do you regard the Holy Spirit to be, and how does he relate to you?

_____

_____

_____

Look up these different Scripture passages: John 14:26, 1 John 4:12-13, and Ephesians 1:13-14.

These passages describe some of the roles of the Holy Spirit in your life. Identify some of them.

John 14:26: The Holy Spirit is…

_____

_____

1 John 4:12-13: The Holy Spirit is…

_____

_____

Ephesians 1:13-14: The Holy Spirit is…

_____

_____

 Video

Now play DVD Session Nine, Part 2, or go back to **www.unshakable truth.com/sg** and click on "Video Menu" and then on "Session Nine, Part 2" to view Josh and Sean discussing this truth for 7 minutes.

||||||||||||||||||||||||||||||||||||||||||||||||||||||||||||||||||||||||||||||||||||||||||||||||||||||||||||

How It Applies

If you have yet to experience the Spirit-filled life, we invite you to do so now. If you feel you have more to learn about walking in the power of the Holy Spirit, we suggest that you read *The Unshakable Truth* book, chapter 39, which is entitled: "How to Live in the Power of the Holy Spirit."

Based on Galatians 5:22-23 and Acts 1:8, what does the Holy Spirit equip you to become and do?

_____

_____

_____

How to Walk in the Spirit

What is our greatest hindrance to walking in the Spirit? Read Galatians 5:16-18,24-25 and Ephesians 4:20-24.

The Holy Spirit wants to live his life continually through you. What do you do to welcome him to do that?

_____

_____

Read Ephesians 4:20-24 and 2 Corinthians 3:18. Do these passages indicate that being like Christ through the power of his Spirit happens instantly or as a process? Give a reason for your answer.

_____

_____

_____

Dr. Bill Bright wrote a booklet on the Holy Spirit. In it he describes a process he calls "spiritual breathing." If you're in a group, someone read aloud what he wrote:

"If you become aware of an area of your life (an attitude or an action) that is displeasing to the Lord, even though you are walking with Him and sincerely desiring

to serve Him, simply thank God that He has forgiven your sins—past, present, and future—on the basis of Christ's death on the cross. Claim His love and forgiveness by faith and continue to have fellowship with Him.

"If you retake the throne of your life through sin—a definite act of disobedience—breathe spiritually. Spiritual Breathing (exhaling the impure and inhaling the pure) is an exercise in faith that enables you to experience God's love and forgiveness."

Exhale: Read 1 John 1:9 and 2:1. What should you do if you sin after becoming a Christian?

_____

_____

_____

When you fail God and are disobedient, and quickly seek his forgiveness with a repentant heart, what is his response to you?

_____

_____

Inhale: Read Ephesians 5:18 and Romans 12:1-2. Exhaling is about confessing. Inhaling is about what in your life?

_____

_____

_____

The more you surrender your desires, dreams, and hopes in life to him, the more he will live his life of power and joy through you. Inhaling is about receiving more and more of him.

Write out your prayer and desire to God about allowing him to be reflected more and more in your life.

_____

_____

_____

Truth Encounter

Read John 17:26. Set aside this time to consider the mystery of the loving relationship within the Trinity—a loving relationship of giving and serving one another. Now reflect on Christ's request for his disciples—that the love between the Father, Son, and Spirit would be in his followers. Consider the wonder of the sovereign God, who has existed for all of eternity and wants to express his love to you and through you to others. This love comes to live inside of you when you trust Christ. And as you walk in the Spirit, his love is expressed through you.

Pause to remember any recent expressions of the Holy Spirit's giving/serving love through you. How have you touched the lives of family members or friends and given a testimony of the Spirit's work of love in your own life?

"I recently had the joy of giving to/serving (who) _____ *by…*

_____

_____

_____ *."*

(For example: "I recently had the joy of serving my grandmother by taking her to the doctor's office. It was a perfect way for me to serve her and let her know that we care for her deeply. She has spent years being a testimony of unconditional love for us. It was a huge blessing to be able to give back to her. I'm sure it was the Spirit's work of love and gratitude in my life that enabled me to see a simple trip to the doctor's office in that way.")

If you are in a group, take turns sharing these reflections with each other, celebrating God's faithfulness and becoming more mindful that God's Spirit is actually involved in expressing his love through you to others.

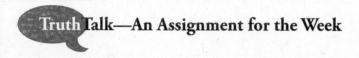

Truth Talk—An Assignment for the Week

As a devotional this week, read Galatians 5 and 6 and practice spiritual breathing. Then look for opportunities to share what you have discovered with others. Consider the following as examples of your TruthTalk with a family member or friend.

1 "During a group study I'm going through, we talked about the importance of how God co-exists as three persons: the Father, the Son, and the Holy Spirit. It's the Holy Spirit who empowers us to love others. God's Spirit has prompted me

to initiate more love and care for _____ by

_____ ."

2 "I've been sensing the Spirit's concern and conviction for my life. I know God wants me to be more…

_____ ."

3 "I've come to a new understanding that God exists as three persons: Father, Son, and Holy Spirit. The relationship between the persons of the Trinity is an amazing testimony of how love works. I've been especially moved by this truth because…

_____ ."

Read chapters 40–43 of *The Unshakable Truth* book this week.

||||||||||||||||||||||||||||||||||||||||||||||||||||||||||||||||||||||||||||||||||||||||||||||||||||||

Close Your Time in Prayer

TRUTH TEN: GOD'S KINGDOM

What Are We Talking About?

Think about the concept of two kingdoms as you read these paragraphs from chapter 40 of *The Unshakable Truth* book.

"While Jesus was on earth he talked a lot about the kingdom of heaven, the kingdom of God. The Roman governor, Pontius Pilate, was trying to get some clarity on that issue when Jesus was brought before him. He asked Jesus if he was the king of the Jews. The governor was trying to determine Jesus' political ambition.

"'Then Jesus answered, "I am not an earthly king. If I were, my followers would have fought when I was arrested by the Jewish leaders. But my Kingdom is not of this world"' (John 18:36). This further confused Pilate. Jesus was not an earthly king? What other kind of king is there? *the governor probably wondered.* He's got a kingdom, but it's not of this world? How odd.

"It is odd unless you understand Jesus' concept of the kingdom. Jesus' kingdom idea was not about toppling the Roman Empire. His opposition wasn't the Romans or even the Jewish leaders. His opposition was Lucifer, his archenemy. You see, once Adam and Eve sinned it was Satan that moved in and made this present world his kingdom, the kingdom of darkness. So Jesus wasn't focused on human governments; he was focused on Satan's world order. Jesus came to earth to reclaim his lost creation and re-establish the circle of relationship between the Godhead (Father, Son, and Holy Spirit) and his human creation. Jesus came to re-establish his kingdom.

"So now two kingdoms exist—the kingdom of this world, with Satan as its king, and the kingdom of heaven with God as its King. That means that we are presently in the midst of a mighty conflict between two kingdoms warring against each other.

"So the conflict isn't really political in nature as Pilate assumed. The struggle isn't even a cultural one. The primary enemy isn't wicked people or evil regimes of this world. The war is between God and his ways and Satan and his ways. And we as followers of Jesus are to be fighting this war alongside Christ. 'For we are not fighting against people made of flesh and blood,' the apostle Paul told us, 'but against the evil rulers and authorities of the unseen world, against those mighty powers of darkness who rule this world, and against wicked spirits in the heavenly realms' (Ephesians 6:12). And when we live out Jesus' kingdom worldview, we are engaging in a mighty spiritual conflict to overthrow Satan's kingdom, the kingdom of this world, and establish Christ's kingdom in its place. By worldview we simply mean what we all assume to be true about the basic makeup of our world. A worldview is like a mental map of reality. We believe certain things about ourselves and God and life, and then we interpret our attitudes and actions through them. Jesus' idea of life and relationships is actually his kingdom worldview."

Can you debate the two differing kingdom worldviews with people like you would, for example, a political or economic philosophy? Read 1 Corinthians 2:12-14.

Why is it often futile to debate spiritual things with people who don't know God?

Because they don't have the understanding
& discernment of the Holy Spirit

What are some examples of how people of the kingdom of the world view life and relationships and you as a citizen of the kingdom of heaven view life and relationships?

Describe two views from Matthew 5:43-45.

Love like Jesus even those who
are not in the same belief as me

"Love y our enemies, pray for them'
worldview: love those who you love

Describe two views from Matthew 5:27-28.

Sin ... it is not only action but thoughts

worldview... action is wrong
don't really think that the
thought may already be sin

Describe two views from Matthew 6:31-33.

Seek God first, + be righteous + all will come + be provided... Do not worry unbeliever... provide those things try for yourself by your means + worry + fret

‖‖

Session Objective

To discover more clearly how our worldview is formed and define what it is for each of us personally.

Video

Now play DVD Session Ten, Part 1, or go back to **www.unshakable truth.com/sg** and click on "Video Menu" and then on "Session Ten, Part 1" to view Josh and Sean introducing this truth for 5 minutes.

1 Corinthians 16:

We are talking about Truth Ten: God's Kingdom

How Do You Answer?

Can you define your worldview and explain how you formed it? _____

If you can, explain in brief what your worldview is and how you formed it. *I see God is @ work + my role is to step in esp. Jesus right now I see a battle + raging in the spiritual realms for the souls of the world. I see God setting the stage for His Jesus return. I am waiting tho.*

Most of us can't clearly define our worldview verbally, even though we all have one. The thing about Jesus' kingdom worldview is that it is a whole new way to see God, ourselves, life, and relationships. It is a view of life that is defined by God and his Word.

Has Jesus' kingdom worldview, as lived out by his followers past or present, made a positive difference in the world? Name some people or groups and their actions toward others that have been honorable and good.

Yes ... all the service organizations and the missionarys + the helpers

Truth Ten: God's Kingdom

We believe the truth that Jesus' kingdom-of-God life and message forms our biblical worldview. It is this biblical worldview that not only provides us an accurate view of God, human history, life, relationships, death, and the world to come, but also a supernatural way to be and live in this present world.

Video

Now play DVD Session Ten, Part 2, or go back to **www.unshakabletruth .com/sg** and click on "Video Menu" and then on "Session Ten, Part 2" to view Josh and Sean discussing this truth for 13 minutes.

How It Applies

"This kingdom worldview—the Way of Jesus—may be spiritual in nature, but it affects every area of life. Jesus' worldview unlocks a very specific way of life, a way of knowing what is really true, a picture of being what God meant us to be, and the power to live that out based on our relationship with God. When we see and live by God's spiritual worldview, it combats darkness, injustice, and evil within the world. And that in turn brings resolution to the physical, economic, social, moral, ethical, and environmental problems of life. In fact, God's new world order, which Jesus spiritually imparts to his followers today, will someday be a permanent and all-pervasive world order established in a new heaven and a new earth where there is no more sin, pain, sorrow, or death. But until the final and permanent kingdom of heaven envelops the kingdom of earth, we are to be his witnesses, the messengers of Jesus' worldview, which is to be lived out for all to see."

The following eight questions will help you clarify your assumptions about life and how you view the world.

1. What or who defines your reality? In other words, what ultimately makes life real and meaningful—is it the material cosmos, your own being, or what? Read Genesis 1:1.

Jesus, people

2. *How does the world exist?* In other words, a) Is the world basically chaotic or orderly? b) Is the world created or naturally formed? c) Is the world randomly functioning or part of a master design? Read Hebrews 1:3.

God created the world to be in His order by His hand & master plan. It is unfolding but Satan steps in & we choose

3. *What is a human being?* In other words, are we a highly complex machine, a highly evolved organism, or what? Read Genesis 1:26.

made in the image of God. created by God to rule over all creatures

4. *Why is it possible to know anything?* In other words, is our learning and knowledge based on survival of the fittest—that is, that the ones who survive have learned the most—or on some other basis? Read John 17:3.

Knowledge is to know God & Jesus. This comes t a relationship with Jesus

5. *How do you know right from wrong?* In other words, are morals determined by human choice, what feels good, cultural consensus, or what? Read Deuteronomy 32:4 and Ecclesiastes 12:13-14.

Through the Holy Spirit coming through God's Word
• Word • Holy Spirit • others teaching

6. *What happens to you after death?* In other words, is death the extinction of a person, the possibility of being reincarnated, the flowing back into nature, or what? Read 1 Corinthians 15:42-43.

our body will be a new spiritual body unperishable, glory, peaceful

7. What is the meaning of human history? In other words, is the purpose of time to make this planet a better place to live, to acquire more knowledge and use it to better humanity, to figure out the grand purpose of history, or what? Read 1 Corinthians 15:20-28 and Revelation 21:3.

To understand + know God + He will abide with us.

8. What core commitments are consistent with your worldview? In other words, is your primary commitment in life to realize your personal potential, give back to society and the planet, live in a world of inner peace within yourself, or what? Read Matthew 22:37 and Matthew 6:33.

Love God with my soul, heart, mind Seek God... pursue Him 1st love... God, my time, my obedience

"The answers to these eight questions form your worldview. It is only a biblical world-view that makes sense out of all the confusion, chaos, and tragedies of the world. While we may not be able to live out our biblical worldview perfectly, <u>God is still at work in us perfecting his will in our lives.</u> We experience his pleasure and joy because living out a biblical worldview ultimately provides the only satisfying answers to the three deepest questions of life:

Who Are You?

"You are a human being created in the image and likeness of a relational God. But you have lost your sense of identity because of your sin, which brought death to your Father-child relationship with your Creator. God took the initiative to bring you back into relationship with him, and because you have trusted in his solution (his Son dying in your stead) you have regained your **identity** as a transformed, born-again child of God. *You have regained your family connection to your Father God.*

Why Are You Here?

"Made alive to God because of Christ, you enjoy a Father-child relationship that is continually conforming you to the image of God's Son. Your **purpose** is to bring glory and honor to your God *by living to please him. You bring him pleasure, he brings you joy.*

Where Are You Going?

"Sin and death, pain and suffering, still exist. Yet God is on a mission to restore all things to his original design. You have joined his mission to proclaim the good news of God's kingdom to come. One day sin and death will be brought to an end. Your destiny is to live eternally with God and your loved ones in a new heaven and a new earth.

"Your biblical worldview gives you a clear sense of your identity, purpose, and destiny in life. As God empowers you to live out your worldview, he completes you, gives you a sense of meaning, and provides you an expectant hope of an eternal future. No other worldview provides so much joy. No other worldview provides such overwhelming evidence that it is true. No other worldview provides for such a glorious future."

Truth Encounter

Read Philippians 3:8.

Our worldview has its origins in a relationship with a Person named Jesus! God's Spirit is at work in you so you might know him, love him, and serve him.

Take the next few moments to reflect on your own recent encounters with Christ and how they have deepened your sense of who he really is.

"Recently, I have come to better know Christ and his (compassion, forgiveness, or something else) _____amazing presence_____ .
I have come to know more of this about our Lord as he has _____

provided for our new home
• people in my life ."

(For example: "Recently, I have come to better know Christ and his acceptance of me. I have come to know more of this about our Lord as he has provided people in my life to accept me in spite of my fears and anxieties.")

If you are in a group, share your response with others. Close this time with verbalized sentence prayers that express your gratitude and praise.

TruthTalk—An Assignment for the Week

Take the time this week to share with two others—friends or family—your identity, purpose, and destiny in life. Refer to this session and share with them who you are, why you are here, and where you are going. As you do, you are joining in Christ's mission to proclaim his kingdom. Consider the following TruthTalk suggestions as a guide.

1 "As a part of a study I've been going through, I have carefully considered my view of the world and how that can become laser-focused when I know Jesus. I've been especially grateful for this renewed perspective because...

_____

_____ ."

2 "The more I come to know Jesus, the more grateful I am for his...

_____

_____

_____ ."

3 "Taking the time to really get to know Jesus has made a huge difference in my life. Knowing him better has changed my...

_____

_____ ."

Read chapters 44–47 of *The Unshakable Truth* book this week.

||||||||||||||||||||||||||||||||||||||||||||||||||||||||||||||||||||||||||||||||||||||||||||||||||||

Close Your Time in Prayer

TRUTH ELEVEN: THE CHURCH

What Are We Talking About?

What is your earliest memory of church? As you grew up, did your perception of the church become negative or positive?

"When I was growing up, my view of the church was…

going each Sunday with Mom & sisters
grew up Catholic, mostly negative."
Sacrificial seeming

How do you think most non-churched people view the Christian church in the United States? What image do most non-churched people have of the church?

Christianity a
Burden and controling and
judgemental

Session Objective

To discover a clearer definition of the true church from Scripture and personally experience how the church is relevant to each of our lives in at least one area.

Video

Now play DVD Session Eleven, Part 1, or go back to **www.unshakable truth.com/sg** and click on "Video Menu" and then on "Session Eleven, Part 1" to view Josh and Sean introducing this truth for 2 minutes.

We are talking about Truth Eleven: The Church

How Do You Answer?

How would you define the Christian church—the church as God intended it?

"I define the church as God meant it to be as...

the hands & feet of Jesus. To bring the good news to the world, to love & serve. But to know Your Word & Truth to stand on Truth"

The true nature of the church is explained in this excerpt from chapter 45 of *The Unshakable Truth* book.

"The late author and Christian historian Dr. Robert Webber passed along this startling quote:

- *'The church started as a missionary movement in Jerusalem.*
- *It moved to Rome and became an institution.*
- *It traveled to Europe and became a culture.*
- *It crossed the Atlantic to America and became a big business.'*

"While there may be some truth to that quote, Christ's true church is still alive and well today. It's true that 'church' organizations and institutions disappoint, and many may have lost their way as God's visible expression of himself. But if you look, you can

find the church active and involved in the world. Bob Roberts Jr., pastor of a mega-church and author of the book Transformation, said he had to travel halfway around the world to see firsthand what the church looked like. He relates this story:

"'I didn't even realize how lost I was until I saw what the church was really supposed to look like. At first, I didn't even recognize it; then I wanted to rationalize it. I had to go halfway around the world to find it—in the persecuted underground house church in Asia. I had heard the stories and statistics, but I had never met anyone face to face. They were nothing like me. They were nothing like any believers I had ever met. Not just culturally, but spiritually they blew me away. Sure, their theology is fuzzy. Some don't even have whole parts of the Bible, only perhaps an entire book or a few passages. But they know God at a depth I never had nor knew anyone else who had.

"'Worship takes on a completely new expression on the other side of the world. No sound systems, no calculated transitions, just sweaty believers crammed together into small rooms, weeping as the Holy Spirit oozes out among them, as I never before experienced. I don't know if they are charismatic or not (all I knew was it wasn't my tongue), but it doesn't matter. No one is getting rich, and no one is fighting for control or position. If there is a favored position, it is the privilege of being the first to die. Living on the edge as they do leaves little room for insincerity or self-promotion. These people are living what I grew up hearing the church should be.

"'Through small, indigenous, underground house church networks, these churches are transforming lives and their cultures. They cannot be stopped. There are too many of them, and they are spreading everywhere, every day. Here's a shocker: Lay-people start these movements, not just those "called" to full-time vocational ministry. Their church planting is the result of transformed lives and not the result of a grand strategy, even though the strategy is grand.'"

Is the above description of the church what you perceive it should be? Why or why not?

Yes! This is how God intended...
relationship with God 1st, then shared
with other believers, expect the power of
the Holy Spirit, serve spread Gospel, serve

Jesus' church exists today as it did in the first century. The process of its expansion is the same. Lives are transformed by Christ's saving power, those lives form a community of hope, love, and care, and they by nature become Jesus' ambassadors to proclaim his kingdom message of love and redemption to the world around them.

There are at least six images the New Testament gives us of Christ's church. Follow along and read the Scripture passages below as Sean describes the church biblically.

Video

Now play DVD Session Eleven, Part 2, or go back to **www.unshakable truth.com/sg** and click on "Video Menu" and then on "Session Eleven, Part 2" to view Josh and Sean discussing this truth for 13 minutes.

Scriptural Images of the Church

Fill in the blanks as you view the video online.

Galatians 6:15-16. The church is _____

_____ .

Ephesians 2:19-20. The church is _____

_____ .

Ephesians 2:33. The church is _____

_____ .

1 Corinthians 3:16. The church is _____

_____ .

Ephesians 5:25-27. The church is _____

_____ .

2 Corinthians 5:18,20. The church is _____

_____ .

Truth Eleven: The Church

We believe the truth that the church is Christ's visible representation on earth, in which each transformed follower of Jesus is made part of his living body to individually and collectively fulfill God's redemptive purpose.

How It Applies

Josh concluded by saying that the authentic church is the body of Christ living out truth in relationship with one another and the world around them. How do we as his body do that?

Read Luke 19:1-9. What was Zacchaeus' profession, and do you think he felt accepted by his people, the Jews (verses 2 and 7)?

_____

_____

What was Jesus' attitude toward Zacchaeus (verse 5)?

_____

_____

How did Jesus respond to this tax collector (verses 9-10)? Note the contrast between Jesus' response and the Jewish response.

_____

_____

_____

Did Jesus meet Zacchaeus' spiritual or human relational need or both?

_____ .

Jesus, the head of the church and our model, consistently met people at the point of their need of the moment, whether it was a spiritual or human need.

Truth Encounter

Read John 13:34-35.

What do these verses say that characterizes Jesus' disciples—his church?

_____

_____

_____

To actually experience a Jesus kind of love in the room right now, someone in the group—anyone—take the initiative and share a recent pleasant experience or memory. It can be anything that brought you a greater sense of love, joy, happiness. (Note: If you are doing this study as an individual and not part of a group, take the time today or later this week to experience this truth with someone. Answer the questions throughout this exercise.)

What is that happy experience or memory?

_____

_____

_____

Read Romans 12:15a. How are we to respond to someone who is happy and rejoicing?

_____

_____

So someone—more than one—rejoice with your friend: Be happy, glad, grateful, and joyful with your friend right now.

What did you, the one with the happy experience or memory, sense when others rejoiced with you?

_____

Read Romans 12:15b. What does feeling sad or mourning with someone look like and sound like?

_____

_____

_____

Mourning with and comforting someone isn't about a pep talk or trying to cheer him or her up. It's about sensing the painful hurt of another and simply sharing in that pain with words like "I'm so sorry you had to go through that" or "I know that must hurt, and I hurt with you." Comfort looks like a warm embrace or a tear trickling down a cheek.

Now someone in the room take the initiative to share a painful experience from the recent past or a painful childhood memory. What is that memory or experience? Share it with the group.

_____

_____

_____

In obedience to Romans 12:15, members of your group mourn with your friend with words and actions of comfort.

"You have just experienced Jesus' love being passed on to one who was happy and one who was sad. The authentic church is where God lives and loves through his people. He has given us Christ's body so we can be equipped for service and pass on his love to others to meet the human and spiritual needs of those around us. As a part of such a church we never have to be alone. Christ is present in our lives through the indwelling presence of God's Holy Spirit, and the members of his body are there to be with us through thick or thin.

"God's church is alive and well today to offer hope. As a living embodiment of Jesus' love it says to each of us and to a needy world (among other things):

- *There is comfort to ease our hurts in life, to provide a shoulder to cry on, and to produce inner healing.*
- *There is attention (care) that communicates that we are so important to God that he died to have a relationship with us, and his church is here to help address all our human and spiritual needs.*
- *There is acceptance that says we are loved for who we are, no matter what.*

105

- *There is* appreciation *that gives praise to us for who we are and what we've done.*
- *There is* support *when we need a helping hand or a shoulder to help us carry a heavy load.*
- *There is* encouragement *when we are struggling with disappointments, failure, or difficulty.*
- *There is* affection *to help us know that through it all, we are truly loved.*
- *There is* approval *that says, 'I am pleased with you.'*
- *There is* security *in times of danger, to remove our fear of the future.*
- *There is* respect *that honors us for what we think and values us for the contribution we bring.*

"The church, Christ's body, is alive and well in order to 'equip God's people to do his work and build up the church, the body of Christ, until we come to such unity in our faith and knowledge of God's Son that we will be mature and full grown in the Lord, measuring up to the full stature of Christ. Then we will no longer be like children, forever changing our minds about what we believe because someone has told us something different or because someone has cleverly lied to us and made the lie sound like the truth. Instead, we will hold to the truth in love, becoming more and more in every way like Christ, who is the head of his body, the church' (Ephesians 4:12-15)."

Truth Talk—An Assignment for the Week

This week, *be* the living church to someone by meeting their need for comfort, support, attention, acceptance—whatever need they have. Follow Jesus' command, "Just as I have loved you, you should love one another" (John 13:34). The following TruthTalk examples may give you some ideas of how to share what you discovered.

1 "In a study I am going through, I am learning about the 'living church' and actually practiced what it might look like to 'be' that kind of church. As part of the church we are to live out Scripture. I learned how one Scripture passage in Romans 12:15 can be experienced right now. Let me explain.

_____

_____."

2 "I'm grateful that God has provided two critical sources to meet our needs. He not only meets our needs for comfort, acceptance, and support himself—he has provided the people of his church to do the same. I'm so grateful for our church because...

_____

_____."

3 "I can't wait to 'be' the church in ways that are more tangible. I'm especially looking forward to...

_____

_____."

Read chapters 48–51 of *The Unshakable Truth* book this week.

〜〜

Close Your Time in Prayer

TRUTH TWELVE: THE RETURN OF CHRIST

What Are We Talking About?

When you think of heaven, what do you envision?

"I think heaven will be like _____

_____

_____. "*

Before heaven becomes a reality for any of us, we must pass through the gateway of death and receive an immortal body. But what key event in history must first take place before heaven is our final home? (Read Acts 1:6-11 and John 14:1-3.)

_____

_____

_____

Session Objective

To gain a better understanding of what God has planned for us and how to continue to store up treasures in heaven.

Video

Now play DVD Session Twelve, Part 1, or go back to **www.unshakable truth.com/sg** and click on "Video Menu" and then on "Session Twelve, Part 1" to view Josh and Sean introducing this truth for 3 minutes.

We are talking about Truth Twelve: The Return of Christ

How Do You Answer?

Without getting into end-times prophecies, what do you think Jesus is ultimately going to do when he returns?

_____

_____

_____

According to 1 Corinthians 15:42-43, what does Jesus have in store for our bodies?

_____

_____

What does Jesus have in store for this earth? Read Isaiah 65:17, 2 Peter 3:13, and Revelation 22:3.

_____

_____

_____

What does Jesus have in store for the devil and for sin and suffering? Read 1 John 3:8 and Revelation 21:4 and 21:27.

_____

_____

_____

Some people think God's children will live in heaven for eternity—meaning we live in God's home. But what does Scripture say—are we going to God, or is God coming to us? (Read Revelation 21:3.)

_____

_____

_____

Consider God's restoration as described in chapter 48 of *The Unshakable Truth* book.

"When Peter asked what was in store for the disciples that followed Jesus, Jesus said, 'At the renewal of all things, when the Son of Man sits on his glorious throne, you who have followed me will also sit on twelve thrones, judging the twelve tribes of Israel' (Matthew 19:28 NIV). Peter later wrote, 'In keeping with his promise we are looking forward to a new heaven and a new earth, the home of righteousness' (2 Peter 3:13 NIV). Jesus also told us that 'when the Son of Man comes in his glory,' he 'will say to those on his right, "Come, you who are blessed by my Father; take your inheritance, the kingdom prepared for you since the creation of the world"' (Matthew 25:31,34 NIV).

"God has not given up on his original plan. He has neither abandoned the idea of a perfect earth, nor has he laid aside his plan for his children to live in a perfect place forever. He has no intention of taking us away to some distant heaven and then destroying this earth he designed to be our home. After his resurrection, Jesus ascended into heaven with a promise to return. He will return and restore this earth to his original design. God's perfect plan is 'to bring all things in heaven and on earth together under one head, even Christ' (Ephesians 1:10 NIV).

"Notice that in the verse above Paul tells us that the earth, as well as heaven, will be under one head. If we who now live on the earth were to be taken into heaven, what would be left on the earth to be brought together under one head? Heaven is God's home. The earth is our home, not only now, but forever, just as God originally intended. And it is Jesus who will eternally bring us together with God and connect

his home with ours. In his revelation, John saw the holy city, the New Jerusalem, coming down from God out of heaven and said, 'Look, the home of God is now among his people! He will live with them, and they will be his people. God himself will be with them' (Revelation 21:3).

"Theologian Randy Alcorn in his book Heaven puts it this way:

"'There will be one cosmos, one universe united under one Lord—forever. This is the unstoppable plan of God. This is where history is headed. When God walked with Adam and Eve in the Garden, Earth was Heaven's backyard. The New Earth will even be more than that—it will be Heaven itself. And those who know Jesus will have the privilege of living there.'

"When God's restoration project is complete we will experience a renewed earth in the perfection of the Garden of Eden. 'No longer will anything be cursed' (Revelation 22:3). No more thorns or thistles to prick our bodies. No more difficulty in getting things to grow. No more 'survival of the fittest' among the animals. For they will all be at peace with one another."

Video

Now play DVD Session Twelve, Part 2, or go back to **www.unshakable truth.com/sg** and click on "Video Menu" and then on "Session Twelve, Part 2" to view Josh and Sean discussing this truth for 15 minutes.

Truth Twelve: The Return of Christ

We believe the truth that Jesus will return to resurrect our lifeless bodies into everlasting bodies, abolish sin, and restore the earth to a perfect world where he will live with us forever and forever.

How It Applies

Christ promised to return to earth, yet his mission to redeem a lost world and restore all things to their original design is not yet accomplished.

Read 2 Peter 3:13-15 and 2 Corinthians 5:18. What does waiting for Christ's return and partnering with him to fulfill his mission look like in your life?

"I'm involved in Christ's mission to reach those around me and the world as I...

_____

_____

_____*."*

Being an effective witness for Christ as we await his return involves a number of things. One of those things is what Jesus referred to as "storing up treasures in heaven." Read Matthew 6:19-21. Specifically identify a number of things you can say, think, or do this week that will store up treasures in heaven:

_____

_____

_____

_____

_____

Truth Encounter

Peter said, "We are looking forward to the new heaven and new earth he has promised, a world where everything is right with God" (2 Peter 3:13). As a closing exercise, answer the following two questions.

Question #1: What are some positive things you are looking forward to in your home in the new heaven and earth?

_____

_____

Question #2: What are some negative things you are so glad will not be part of your new home with God? *Note:* Have someone in your group write down those negative things on a separate piece of paper. If you are doing this study apart from a group go ahead and do the same thing.

_____

_____

Instructions

Now, ask the person with the list of negative things on it to crumple it up and throw it on the floor at the appropriate time as someone in your group reads the following passage. The person reading the verses will give a cue when the paper is to be crumpled up and thrown to the floor. Follow this exercise even if you are doing this study individually as a reinforcement to this Scripture passage.

"We are pressed on every side by troubles, but we are not crushed and broken. We are perplexed, but we don't give up and quit. We are hunted down, but God never abandons us. We get knocked down, but we get up again and keep going...We know that the same God who raised our Lord Jesus will also raise us with Jesus and present us to himself along with you. All of these things are for your benefit...That is why we never give up. Though our bodies are dying, our spirits are being renewed every day. For our present troubles are quite small and won't last very long. Yet they produce for

us an immeasurably great glory that will last forever! So we don't look at the troubles we can see right now [cue the person to crumple the paper and throw it to the floor]; *rather, we look forward to what we have not yet seen. For the troubles we see will soon be over, but the joys to come will last forever"(2 Corinthians 4:8-9,14-18).*

Take a few moments and praise God for his mercy, strength, love, and provisions, and for his promise to one day give us "a world where everything is right with God." (Write these praise notes down.)

_____

_____

_____

_____

_____

TruthTalk—An Assignment for the Week

Take your "storing up treasures in heaven" list you wrote out in this session and put them to practice this week. Here are some suggested TruthTalk examples to share with your family and friends.

1 "In my study time this week I learned about God's plan for restoration and his ultimate plan for our future. I was reminded of how our loving God…

_____

_____

I was also reminded of how I can't wait to be a part of…

_____ ."

2 "The more I see the state of our world, the more I want to be a better (support, witness, testimony, or something else) for…

_____ ."

3 "Since all the 'things' of this world won't last, it makes me want to become a better…

_____."

Note: We Need Your Help

To help us serve you better in the future, would you take a few minutes before the close of your session to fill out the "Evaluation Form" on page 123? This will enable us to know what is working and how we can make future series a better equipping tool for you. Just fill it out and drop it in the mail to the address provided. Thank you.

||||||||||||||||||||||||||||||||||||||||||||||||||||||||||||||||||||||||||||||||||||||||||||||||||||||||||||||||||||||||||

Close Your Time in Prayer

GROUP LEADER'S GUIDE

What Is It that You Hope to Accomplish?

Going through *The Unshakable Truth Study Guide* with a small group means you will have approximately 12 hours of interaction with them. What, realistically, can be accomplished during that time? With God working through you, our prayer is that each participant can get an introduction to the foundations of the faith so they can gain a clearer understanding of what Christianity really means. During your time together each person will be challenged to live out the true faith in relationship to their families and the world around them.

Imagine asking your adult group these questions: *What defines the Christian faith? What does it really mean to be a true follower of Christ? What are the core beliefs that make a true disciple of Jesus?* Most Christians can't answer those questions correctly. And without a clear understanding of what Christianity is, we all will struggle both to live out our faith and pass it on to our families and the world around us.

This doesn't mean, of course, that your group doesn't have answers. The question is, do they have *biblical* answers? A recent study among Christians revealed that 81 percent said the essence of the Christian faith was "trying harder to follow the rules described in the Bible." Even pastors struggle with this issue. Amazingly, 75 percent of Christian leaders were not able to define clearly the core of Christianity and the process of spiritual maturity.* Polls and our own experience tell us that there is a lot of confusion among Christians about what the essence of Christianity actually is.

The Christian faith is more than a set of teachings or laws to govern our actions. It is about a relationship—a relationship lost early in human history and a relationship

---

* Barna Research Group, Barna.org Web site article #264, "Many Churchgoers and Faith Leaders Struggle to Define Spiritual Maturity" (Ventura, CA: The Barna Research Group, Ltd., 2008), 1, 3.

re-established by God's intervention. And in experiencing this reconnected God-human relationship, a person sees the whole of life illuminated through a new lens that clarifies and defines everything we know and experience.

Christianity is about who we are and how we relate to God, what we believe about him, how we gain a relationship with him, and how living in relationship with him defines all our other relationships. This is the way God designed us from the beginning—for relationship with him. Therefore, it is crucial that we know how God intends for us to relate to him. To put a succinct definition to the Christian faith that forms our worldview, we could say it is *a way of knowing and being and living in right relationship with God, ourselves, others, and the world around us.* It is Christ's "way" that we must regain and recapture; and when we live in that "way," our lives take on purpose and meaning.

This study guide is based on Josh and Sean McDowell's book *The Unshakable Truth.* And in that book the authors identify 12 core truths of Christianity from Scripture that unlock the secret to our relationship with God and one another. During your study you will touch on each of those truths in order to gain a deeper understanding of them so you can relate them to life and relationships. Consider this study as a foundational step in understanding the true nature of Christianity.

Yet *The Unshakable Truth Study Guide* should be seen as an introductory course. The follow-up or companion course is *TruthWalk*—a comprehensive small-group series that devotes five sessions to each truth. TruthWalk is like a Christian catechism to equip your group for a lifelong pattern of spiritual and relational growth. For more information on the TruthWalk go to www.HarvestHousePublishers.com/TruthWalk.

How to Use the Study Guide

The Unshakable Truth Study Guide is designed to be used interactively by a group and by individuals as well. An individual can certainly benefit by going through it alone; however, more can be experienced and accomplished in a group context.

Each group participant needs a copy of the study guide. (The study guide is not intended to be shared by couples.) Order enough copies so each person attending your group can have one. They can be obtained through your local Christian supplier or by calling the publisher at 1-800-547-8979. Or go online to Harvest HousePublishers.com/UnshakableTruth. It is wise to order a few extra copies to cover individuals who may show up at later sessions. Your church may decide to provide the study guides, or you may want to ask each participant to pay something toward the purchase of their resources.

The book *The Unshakable Truth* is the companion to the study experience. You will want to recommend that each participant read a selection of chapters between sessions. Therefore, consider adding this resource to your order of study guides. Couples can share in the reading of the book, so one book per couple will suffice. You may order the book from your local Christian supplier or by contacting Harvest House Publishers as noted above.

To enhance your group experience there are two optional ways to view videos of Josh and Sean McDowell discussing each truth:

1. You can go to a special website (www.unshakabletruth.com/sg) to view 15 to 17 minutes of teaching per session from Josh and Sean at no cost.
2. You can purchase a high-resolution DVD more suitable for group use. The DVD contains 12 sessions—the same sessions available on the website. Either way this video feature provides an enhanced study experience for you and your group.

On the website mentioned above, you will also find materials to help you promote your small-group meetings, for example, bulletin inserts, postcards, posters, and so on. There is also a sermon a pastor can give to highlight the need for us as Christians to be grounded in the foundations of the faith. You will find this web link to be a valuable resource in conducting *The Unshakable Truth* study within your group.

Each session of this guide is divided into eight areas:

- **What are we talking about?**

  Usually, each session opens with someone in your group reading a selected paragraph or two drawn from *The Unshakable Truth* book. This is followed by questions posed to your group for interactive discussion. Notes are to be taken and written down in the spaces provided in the study guide.

- **Session objective**

  This simply identifies the outcome you are focused on or the desired objective for your group session.

- **Play the DVD or connect to the online video segment (usually about 3 to 5 minutes)**

  You will note that the address www.unshakabletruth.com/sg is given within the study guide to use if you do not have the high-resolution DVD. It enables you to view Josh McDowell and his son, Sean, as they teach on the truth of each session. Check out this web address first. Click on "Video Menu" and then "Session One, Part 1" to sample a viewing. Be sure to have your computer set up for showing the videos at each group meeting. Or if you are using the DVD, check out your DVD player ahead of time.

Your first video showing will always follow the statement of your group objective. The introductory few minutes with Josh and Sean end with "on-the-street interviews" of people answering a question pertinent to the session topic. You will then go back to the study guide section "How Do You Answer?"

- **How do you answer?**

This section of the study guide allows you to prompt your group on how they would answer the question posed to the people "on the street." Your interaction then leads to a clear definition of the truth you are discussing, with a printed statement of "We believe the truth that…"

- **Play the DVD or connect again to the web video (usually about 10 to 12 minutes)**

The second part of the video opens with the on-the-street interviews again, followed by Josh and Sean responding with answers. This segment provides insights and teaching by the McDowell team for your group to interact around—usually 10 to 12 minutes in length. You will then be directed back to your guide at the "How It Applies" section.

- **How it applies**

This is where the truth meets living. This section offers a time to share how the specific truth being discussed is to be reflected in your relationships—in your attitudes and actions. Here you experience an exercise called "Truth Encounter" that helps you put the truth into practice.

- **TruthTalk—an assignment for the week**

Here you encourage your group to "talk the truth" with others and practice some aspect of the truth in daily life during the week. This application may be related to a devotional time with God or living the truth out in relationship with a friend or family member. In every case we will provide some ideas on how to share the truth with family and friends. You will also want to encourage participants to read at least four chapters of *The Unshakable Truth* book prior to each session. The chapter assignments are identified in this section.

- **Close your time in prayer**

  While closing in prayer may seem like the expected thing to do, we encourage you to make praying together a very intentional exercise. Pray as a group that the truth you have encountered will become real, alive, and active in your lives throughout the week. Remember, Truth has a name, and his name is Jesus. Use your prayer time to confess to God and express your desire to live more like Christ. Praying as a group is an important part of making your group experience come alive in each person's heart and life.

||||||||||||||||||||||||||||||||||||||||||||||||||||||||||||||||||||||||||||||||||||||||||||||||||||||||||||||||||||||

Healthy Discussion that Leads to Living the Truth

Biblical truth by its very nature is meant to be lived out in relationships. Talking about the truth within your group is good, but healthy discussion is that which encourages or challenges a person to live the truth out in his or her life. Following are some suggestions in guiding your group discussion to that end.

1. *Don't be afraid of silence.* Some group leaders make the mistake of asking a thought-provoking question and then, when no one answers immediately, moving on too quickly to the next question. The wise leader will try to create an atmosphere in which careful thought is encouraged—by the wise use of silence. Allow a brief time for thought after each question if necessary, then signal for someone to speak up by simply asking, "Anybody?" or "Someone finish your thought out loud."

2. *Let discussion follow its own path without letting the group stray too far.* Don't be in a hurry to move to the next question in the study guide if the discussion is moving forward. But be careful not to let your participants get off on tangents not related to the topic of discussion.

3. *As often as possible, follow a comment with another question.* After a person has made an observation, ask, "Can you think of an example?" or ask how the rest of the group responds.

4. *Don't feel obligated to ask all (or exclusively) the questions in the*

study guide. If your group's time is limited, highlight the questions you wish to ask. Add questions suited to your own group as discussion develops.

5. *When it's practical, "prime the pump" of discussion by planting questions with the most vocal, well-spoken participants.* If your group is slow to start discussions, jot one or two questions onto index cards and give them to some of your most vocal group members before the session, asking them to be ready to offer comments if others don't jump in quickly. You may also ask several confident individuals if they will allow you to call them by name to answer a question if the discussion begins to lag.

6. *Seek attitudinal and behavioral responses.* Don't seek "right" answers as much as truthful discussion. Don't just probe what your group thinks about a truth, but how they respond to a truth attitudinally or behaviorally. The idea is to search out where each person is on their spiritual journey. This isn't to say that wrong attitudes or actions should be agreed with or condoned, it simply means you are creating an atmosphere of transparency and safety where people can open up and be honest with God and their spiritual family.

7. *Finally, refer frequently to Scripture as your baseline.* You will notice that every truth cited is a biblical truth, so Scripture passages are liberally referred to throughout this study guide. While opinions may vary on a lot of issues, encourage your group to answer the question, "What is *God's* opinion on this issue?" And if your participants are to discover what God's position is on these truths, his Word is where they must turn. Scripture is your baseline for revealing his truth.

Your role as a group leader or facilitator is significant. May God use your gifts to his glory as you encourage your group to seek him and allow him to live his truth through their lives.

We Need Your Input

We need your feedback as you go through this process. Will you take the time to fill out the "Evaluation Form" on the next page after you have completed this study experience with your group? It will help us know how to better serve you. Thank you.

The Unshakable Truth™ *Study Guide*

EVALUATION FORM

1. Did you do this study as an individual or in a group? _____

2. If in a group, how many on average participated? _____

3. Did you read all or a portion of *The Unshakable Truth* book? _____

4. On a scale of 1 to 10 (10 being the highest) how would you rate the teaching value of Josh and Sean's presentations? _____

5. Did you purchase the DVD, use the web links, or neither? _____

6. If applicable, was your experience connecting to the web and viewing the videos acceptable? Explain.

   _____

   _____

7. On a scale of 1 to 10 (10 being the highest) how would you rate:

   a) the quality and usefulness of the study guide? _____

   b) the responsiveness and interaction of those in your group? _____

8. To what degree did this course deepen your practical understanding of the Christian faith?

   ☐ Little ☐ Somewhat ☐ Rather considerably

Please give any comments you feel would be helpful to us.

_____

_____

_____

_____

Please mail to: Josh McDowell Evaluation
                PO Box 4126
                Copley, OH 44321

More Resources from Josh McDowell

Throughout Josh and Sean McDowell's book *The Unshakable Truth*, you will find many mentions of *Beyond Belief to Convictions* (from Tyndale House Publishers) and *The New Evidence That Demands a Verdict* (from Thomas Nelson Publishers), as well as much material adapted from them. These two books make great companions to the one you're now holding.

Beyond Belief to Convictions will help you counter the distorted view this generation has about God and the truth. It specifically focuses on how you can instill biblical convictions in the young people you know and love—to help them stand strong in the face of today's culture. To obtain this book, visit your local Christian bookstore or go to www.TyndaleHousePublishers.com.

The New Evidence That Demands a Verdict is a comprehensive reference text on the evidence for the Christian faith. It will equip you with a relevant, ready defense for this decade and beyond. (It includes *Evidence That Demands a Verdict I* and *II* updated in one easy-reference volume.) Visit your local Christian bookstore or go to www.Thomas NelsonPublishers.com.

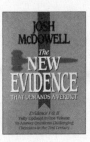

Other Harvest House Books
by Sean McDowell

Apologetics for a New Generation
A Biblical and Culturally Relevant Approach to Talking About God
Sean McDowell

This generation's faith is constantly under attack from the secular media, skeptical teachers, and unbelieving peers. You may wonder, *How can I help?*

Working with young adults every day, Sean McDowell understands their situation and shares your concern. His first-rate team of contributors shows how you can walk members of the new generation through the process of...

- formulating a biblical worldview and applying scriptural principles to everyday issues

- articulating their questions and addressing their doubts in a safe environment

- becoming confident in their faith and effective in their witness

The truth never gets old, but people need to hear it in fresh, new ways. Find out how you can effectively share the answers to life's big questions with a new generation.

Understanding Intelligent Design
Everything You Need to Know in Plain Language
William A. Dembski and Sean McDowell

"Understanding Intelligent Design *is the best book of its type.*"
J.P. Moreland
Author and Distinguished Professor of Philosophy, Biola University

The prevailing mind-set in our schools and in the media is that everything we see came into being strictly by accident. But in this user-friendly resource, William Dembski and Sean McDowell show that many scientists are now admitting that this viewpoint is not based on facts.

Understanding Intelligent Design clearly shows what the best information is revealing—that our existence is not an accidental by-product of nature but the clear result of intelligent design.